Executive Briefing

Controlling Software Development

Lawrence H. Putnam
Ware Myers

IEEE Computer Society Press
Los Alamitos, California

Washington • Brussels • Tokyo

Library of Congress Cataloging-in-Publication Data

Putnam, Lawrence H.
    Executive Briefing: Controlling software development / Lawrence H.
    Putnam, Ware Myers.
       p.   cm.
    Includes bibliographical references.
    ISBN 0-8186-7452-0
    1. Computer software—Development—Management.   I. Myers, Ware.
II. Title.
QA76.76.D47P865   1996
005.1′ 068—dc20

                                         95-52100
                                         CIP

IEEE Computer Society Press
10662 Los Vaqueros Circle
P.O. Box 3014
Los Alamitos, CA 90720-1264

IEEE Computer Society Press Order Number BR07452
Library of Congress Number 95-52100
ISBN 0-8186-7452-0

Additional copies may be ordered from:

IEEE Computer Society Press Customer Service Center 10662 Los Vaqueros Circle P.O. Box 3014 Los Alamitos, CA 90720-1264 Tel: +1-714-821-8380 Fax: +1-714-821-4641 Email: cs.books@computer.org	IEEE Service Center 445 Hoes Lane P.O. Box 1331 Piscataway, NJ 08855-1331 Tel: +1-908-981-1393 Fax: +1-908-981-9667 mis.custserv@computer.org	IEEE Computer Society 13, avenue de l'Aquilon B-1200 Brussels BELGIUM Tel: +32-2-770-2198 Fax: +32-2-770-8505 euro.ofc@computer.org	IEEE Computer Society Ooshima Building 2-19-1 Minami-Aoyama Minato-ku, Tokyo 107 JAPAN Tel: +81-3-3408-3118 Fax: +81-3-3408-3553 tokyo.ofc@computer.org

Assistant Publisher: Matt Loeb
Technical Editor: Mohamed Fayad
Acquisitions Assistant: Cheryl Smith
Advertising/Promotions: Tom Fink
Production Editor: Lisa O'Conner
Cover Design: Alex Torres

The Institute of Electrical and Electronics Engineers, Inc.

Table of Contents

Preface

The book you now hold in your hands is aimed primarily at executives—in fact, at executives with no particular background in software.

This audience includes vice presidents with responsibility for several functional areas, one of which is software; division general managers directing all the functions within a profit center; and chief executive officers. You are all experienced executives. You have risen to a level where you direct functions in addition to the one in which you had your own early experience. You did not yourself, we assume, come up through the software function, but you now have it within your jurisdiction. You have no great grasp of software technology, but you have come to appreciate that you have a problem child on your hands.

We contend that a general executive without professional experience in software development can oversee this function. Obviously, in the limited time a busy executive life allows, you cannot learn the technology of this field in any detail. It is possible, however, to sort out the knowledge you need to operate effectively at your level. In this executive briefing, we help you do that.

There are two aspects of software development that the executive needs to be concerned with. One is the progress of individual projects. Are they being completed on time and within budget? Is the resulting product reliable?

The other is the long-run improvement of the software process. Is your organization's ability to develop software improving year by year? Are you matching the progress being made by your competitors? As software becomes a greater part of the operating cost of enterprises, the ability to improve your process becomes a competitive advantage. Conversely, the inability to keep up leads to the corporate graveyard.

Now, how do you manage the first aspect, project progress, at the executive level? Well, the same as you manage other functions. In essence, you pick attributes to measure, measure them, keep accessible records of the measurements, use the records to estimate schedule and budget of new projects, control against the estimate, and make course corrections when actuals vary from estimates.

Unfortunately, software development does not progress in accordance with the rather simple rules that govern most functions. That is why software projects run beyond delivery dates by many months; overrun budgets, often significantly; and are even canceled about one-quarter of the time. Consequently, you need help to find your way through this thicket. You don't have to learn about structured design or object-oriented programming, but you do have to find the process metrics that actually work.

The second aspect, process improvement, can be reduced to the same executive framework. You measure the efficiency of your present process, invest some money to improve it, and remeasure its efficiency. If the efficiency has increased, great. Invest some more money—with confidence.

Again, how to accurately measure process productivity is not obvious. Many of the measures that have been used in the past have proved to be grossly inaccurate. You need help. A good metric lets you see if your technical people are doing the right things and doing them well. Moreover, it lets them know too.

In this briefing, we deal with software development—at both the project-control level and the process-investment level—in the degree of detail (namely, not much) that the overburdened executive has time to accommodate. For executives with experience in software development who are in immediate charge of a software organization, we suggest our earlier books, *Measures For Excellence: Reliable Software on Time, Within Budget* (Prentice Hall, 1992) and *Software Management: Planning, Reliability, and Process Improvement* (to be published by the IEEE Computer Society Press in 1996). They cover the subject at a more technical level.

To communicate the essentials about the management of software development to executives takes, first, knowledge about software itself and, second, insight into what executives need to know about it. One of us (Putnam) has been researching software estimating, project control, and software process investment since the mid-1970s. Out of this work has evolved the life-cycle management system that this book describes generally (and the referenced books describe more fully).

Putnam performed the initial analysis from the vantage point of Special Assistant to the Commanding General of what was then the Army Computer Systems Command. Thus, from the very beginning, he has viewed software problems from a top-management aspect. This Command, numbering about 1,700 people at the time, developed the software that operates the logistic, personnel, financial, force-accounting, and facilities-engineering functions at worldwide Army installations.

A graduate of the U.S. Military Academy at West Point, with an MS in physics from the U.S. Naval Post Graduate School in Monterey, California, Putnam had management experience with troops early in his career. His knowledge of the theory of management was enhanced at the Command and General Staff College. His understanding of the practical problems of top-level management was extended by four years in the Office of the Director of Management Information Systems and Assistant Secretary of the Army at Headquarters, Department of the Army.

Since 1978, he has been president of Quantitative Software Management, Inc., McLean, Virginia. While QSM is small, it faces the same variety of problems that any independent business entity does. In particular, "I never have enough time to get everything done I would like to do," he says. His personal consulting relationships with scores of top executives of major corporations have given him a keen appreciation of the personal time constraints under which they must operate.

Ware Myers is a graduate of Case Institute of Technology, with an MS in management from the University of Southern California. For many years he was a member of the engineering staff in high-technology corporations, notably Scientific Data Systems and its successor company, Xerox Data Systems, in California. During much of this time he was also a lecturer in engineering organization and administration in the School of Engineering, University of California at Los Angeles. Since 1976, he has been a consulting writer for several major corporations and a contributing editor of *Computer* and

IEEE Software magazines, published by the IEEE Computer Society in Los Alamitos, California. In this capacity he has had the opportunity to talk at length with executives at many levels.

Another formative influence was serving as volunteer treasurer (in effect, chief financial officer) of several nonprofit organizations. Myers found that other board members tended to focus on the delights of spending money for well-meaning purposes, while the treasurer, always conscious of the limited funds coming in, had to be the restraining hand.

Together we hope that we have acquired enough years of experience with the problems of software development and the constraints that limit management to enable us to persuade you that you can control software development and process improvement.

Lawrence H. Putnam
Ware Myers
1996

Chapter 1

Something Old,
Something New

The basic capital resource, the fundamental investment, but also the cost center of a developed economy, is the knowledge worker who puts to work what he has learned in systematic education, that is, concepts, ideas, and theories, rather than the man who puts to work manual skill or muscle.

Peter F. Drucker[1]

Software development is a new field of work. As an organized, group activity, it is less than four decades old. However, work is not new. People have been doing it back into prehistory. Even knowledge-based work—of which software development is a subdivision—goes back a long way. One can think of priests in antiquity, playwrights and philosophers in ancient Greece, and engineers in ancient Rome.

Planning Work Is Not New

As soon as some form of activity becomes work, the person doing it becomes interested in how many personhours it will take, how much calendar time to plan on, what the cost will be, and what the product can sell for. An artisan in the Middle Ages might have drawn a diagram like Figure 1.1A. This diagram represents three factors in the work situation:

(1) the number of people employed in the artisan's shop—at first, just the artisan, then one or two apprentices, and finally, with a severe drop in business, just the artisan again;

(2) the time period, or schedule, over which the work is being done;

(3) the persondays (or personmonths), which we will call effort, represented by the area under the people line.

1

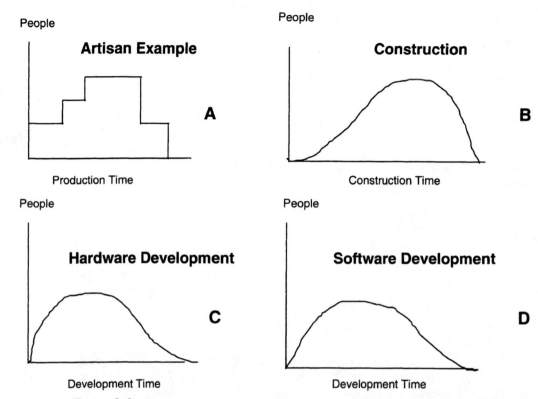

Figure 1.1 People working over time is fundamental to (A) producing manufactured products, (B) constructing buildings or infrastructure, (C) developing hardware or systems, and (D) developing software.

In addition, the artisan would have wanted to know three other numbers not represented on this diagram. One would be the production rate at which shoes could be made. The second, since the artisan was making a physical product, would be the cost of the leather and other raw materials. The third would be the price at which the shoes could sell. Knowing these numbers, the artisan could make enough to live on, support the apprentices, and continue in business. Artisans solved problems like this without knowing how to read, write, or use Arabic numbers.

The artisan's shop was distinguished by three characteristics. First, what we might call the *knowledge work* was done before point zero on production time. That is, the shoes had been designed and the shoemaking process had been devised back in antiquity. Second, the shoemaking process was quite fixed. The artisan did not expect to make continuous improvements in it. It went on generation after generation with little change. Third, production went on indefinitely. The artisan, after a lifetime's work, was succeeded by the senior apprentice. The production process did not have an end.

Today, this simple scenario has evolved into more complicated production planning in large manufacturing plants, but the same three characteristics are generally true of manufacturing production. Again, the product is designed and the machinery and methods to build it are put in place before production starts. Today, we might expect to make improvements in the production process as we go along, but generally these improvements would be incremental. They would not seriously affect production scheduling. Similarly, production continues indefinitely—at least until the automobile accelerator replaces the buggy whip. Under these circumstances management has experience, production rates, costs, and, in general, much data on which to base its plans.

Another work pattern that began in antiquity, the construction project, differs from production in several respects. First, it has a beginning and an end. Second, it is not repetitive. It begins with design, for each structure is different. Only a few architects and draftsmen are needed at this stage, as shown in Figure 1.1B. As physical construction gets under way, the number of people employed increases and reaches a peak. As most of the trades complete their portion of the work, the number of people needed declines and at some point construction ends.

With the beginning of the Industrial Revolution about 200 years ago, the pace of change picked up. The design of something larger and less familiar than a shoe, such as a steamboat, railway, electric utility, or telephone system, began to employ large teams of people. A pattern of hardware development emerged. For instance, in the early years of the 20th century, Henry Gantt invented a chart that showed the sequence of work operations. Then, in the 1950s, the U.S. Navy along with Booz, Allen, and Hamilton developed PERT (Program Evaluation and Review Technique) to plan and control development projects.

At about the same time, Peter V. Norden of the IBM Development Laboratory, in Poughkeepsie, New York, was developing his life-cycle manpower model[2]. It projected manpower needs over a hardware project's development period, as shown in Figure 1.1C. Since manpower is a large fraction of total cost in development, the model could also forecast the expenditure rate. Norden found that this manpower curve could also be represented by an algebraic equation, enabling a manager or an estimator to make useful computations involving project duration and effort.

The equation, named after the 19th century physicist, Lord Rayleigh, is:

$$y = 2Kate^{-at^2}$$

where:

y = manpower rate at each point on curve
  (such as people per month)
K = effort (such as personmonths), which is the area under the curve
t = development time
a = a constant governing the time to peak manpower

In the 1970s, Lawrence H. Putnam applied Norden's concepts to software development, as shown in Figure 1.1D[3]. Software development follows a pattern essentially the same as that of construction and hardware development. In the late 1970s, Putnam implemented his ideas in a software tool called SLIM (Software LIfe cycle Management).

Management Control Is Based on Five Numbers

In a fundamental sense, only five numbers are needed to plan and carry out work. "The fewer controls needed," Peter Drucker observed, "the more effective they will be"[1]. These numbers are:

(1) A measure of the quantity to be produced. In production, for example, it is the number of units to be manufactured. In software development, the measures of quantity most widely used are source lines of code and function points (that is, functions such as input or output).

(2) An indication of the length of calendar time, or schedule, to produce the desired number of units or, in the case of construction or development, to complete the project.

(3) A measure of the cost of production. In the case of hardware or software development, where the cost of materials is small, cost is much the same as effort (or personmonths). Essentially, cost is equal to effort multiplied by an overhead ratio or labor rate.

(4) An indication of the quality of the product or project result. In the case of a hardware product, this number might be the number passing final inspection. In software, it is often the number of defects.

(5) A measure of the productivity of the activity. In the case of production, this measure might be as simple as the number of units per personhour.

How to measure these five quantities is well known in the case of manufacturing and construction, less well known in the case of hardware development, and still subject to differences of opinion in the case of software development. The measurement of schedule and effort in software development presents problems of standardization and organizational discipline, but, in principle, organizations can do it.* The measurement of productivity, quantity, and quality requires a fresh approach. Outlining this approach is one of the main purposes of this book.

---

*Schedule and effort measure calendar time and personmonths devoted to *main build*. This term refers to the principal software construction phase, starting at detailed logic design; continuing through coding, unit testing, subsystem testing, integration, and system testing; and concluding with release, or delivery to the customer.

It is necessary to measure these five quantities because they are fundamental to the basic activities of management. They are the basis for planning the project and this plan is then the basis for key management activities:

(1) Providing the cost input to the price bid to a customer or user;

(2) Establishing the delivery date;

(3) Supplying people with the appropriate skills, equipment, tools, and the like at the times spelled out in the plan;

(4) Providing a baseline against which management can monitor progress and institute corrective action;

(5) Holding managers accountable. In the absence of a realistic plan, accountability is only hypothetical.

Process Improvement Is Urgent

The plan meets the needs of current business operations, but there is a further dimension. Business is not standing still—software technology is advancing rapidly, the business environment is changing, and competitors are improving their ability to produce software—factors that lead to your need to improve your software process.

". . . work, precisely because it is a process rather than an individual operation, needs a built-in control," Drucker advised back in 1973, referring to knowledge work at a time when software development was in its childhood. "It needs a feedback mechanism which both senses unexpected deviations and with them the need to change the process, and maintains the process at the level needed to obtain the desired results."

To improve a process, you must first have a process. The large percentage of organizations that the Software Engineering Institute relegates to its Capability Maturity Level 1, Initial Level (sometimes called ad hoc, or even chaotic) suggests that these software developers do lack an established process. At any rate, when you have a process, you can analyze it and find improvements. Generally, making improvements takes capital for workstations and software tools and money for training. When all goes well, these funds are recovered in the form of savings from the subsequently less costly operation. You can figure the return on investment and then feel confident in financing further improvements.

Estimators call estimating the main build as a whole, macro-estimating. In contrast, estimators term estimating from the bottom up, via work breakdown schedules, PERT diagrams, and the like, *micro-estimating.* This book deals with macro-estimating.

Prior to the main build are two preliminary phases: (1) concept definition (also called feasibility study), including requirements definition; (2) high-level or functional design, including requirements analysis.

Following the main build comes a fourth phase: all the activities following delivery, such as acceptance testing, installation, correction of defects found after delivery, and enhancement to meet changing circumstances—elements sometimes called maintenance.

Something Old

The management principles outlined in this chapter are not new. You can find them in books by Peter Drucker and other management experts. Norden's ideas on development schedules are nearly 40 years old. Putnam's software life cycle model is nearly 20 years old. It has been out long enough to find application in more than 300 organizations, including American Management Systems, Fairfax, Va.; Boeing Computer Services, Vienna, Va.; Chemical Bank, New York, N.Y.; Digital Equipment Corp., The Netherlands; Electronic Data Systems, Dallas, Texas; GTE; Hughes Aircraft Co., Fullerton, Calif.; IBM, Hursley, U.K.; Intel, Provo, Utah; and so on through the alphabet.

Something New

What is new is that these principles have to be applied to the new area of software development, itself only 40 or 50 years old. In particular, as an executive responsible for software operations, you need a means for measuring productivity, a subject we consider in the next chapter. Moreover, you need a means of measuring the quantity of software product, considered in Chapter 3, and you need a means of measuring product quality, the topic of Chapter 4. With productivity, quantity, and quality nailed down, you can plan and estimate software projects accurately. With this plan as the baseline, you can control execution. Moreover, with measures for productivity and quality, you have feedback numbers for gauging process improvement.

> *The manager . . . has to slough off yesterday and to render obsolete what already exists and is already known. He has to create tomorrow.*[1]
>
> *Peter F. Drucker*

[1] P.F. Drucker, *Management: Tasks, Responsibilities, Practices,* Harper & Row, New York, 1973.

[2] P.V. Norden, "Useful Tools for Project Management," in *Operations Research in Research Development,* B.V. Dean, ed., John Wiley & Sons, New York, 1963.

[3] L.H. Putnam, "A General Empirical Solution to the Macro Software Sizing and Estimating Problem," *IEEE Trans. Software Eng.,* Vol. SE-4, No. 4, July 1978, pp. 345–361.

Chapter 2

The Key Metric:
Process Productivity

We are slowly developing measurements, though still quite primitive ones, for the productivity of knowledge-based and service work.

Peter F. Drucker[1]

To plan work, an artisan in the Middle Ages needed to know the production rate, measured in, say, shoes per week. In a modern production plant, a manager also needs to know the production rate. It may be complicated by problems of material supply, machine capacity, occasional breakdowns, slowdowns, and strikes, but the basic need remains. Similarly, a software manager needs to know the rate at which his or her organization can produce software.

The first metric software managers hit upon was lines of code per personmonth. Experience has shown that it is not an accurate measure of production rate. Using it, projects often overrun schedule and cost targets. Even today, however, many software organizations are still using it.

Management-Number Relationships Are Nonlinear

The underlying reason for the weakness of lines of code per personmonth as a measure of the software production rate is that the relationships between quantity and schedule, effort, and defects are nonlinear, as illustrated in Figure 2.1. Using lines of code per personmonth as a production metric assumes a linear relationship. These diagrams show data from hundreds of software projects in all kinds of applications—real time, engineering systems, and business systems.

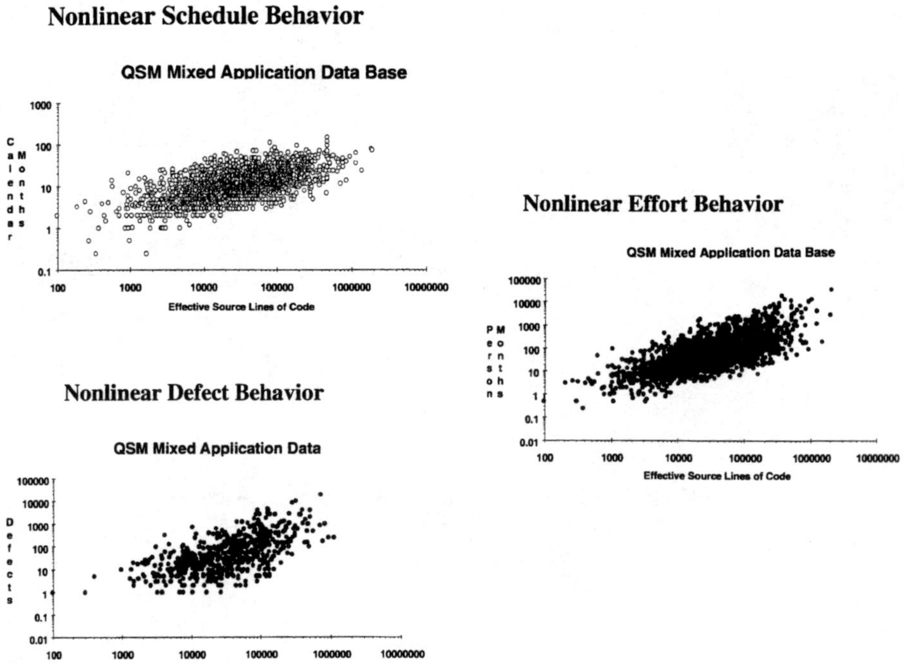

Nonlinear Schedule Behavior

QSM Mixed Application Data Base

Nonlinear Effort Behavior

QSM Mixed Application Data Base

Nonlinear Defect Behavior

QSM Mixed Application Data

Figure 2.1   Three management numbers—schedule in months, manpower in personmonths, and defects—increase as the size of a software project grows. The wide dispersion of the data points in all three cases suggests that the relationships are not simple linear ones.

The diagrams show that the length of the schedule, the personmonths of effort required, and the total number of defects all increase with the size of the project, measured in source lines of code. We could draw a straight line through the data points, representing the mean of the project data. However, because both the horizontal and vertical scales are logarithmic, the relationships are actually nonlinear. In consequence, software estimating is more complicated than the cobbler's linear relationship: shoes per personweek times number of personweeks.

Moreover, while we could draw a mean line through the data points on Figure 2.1, many points are far above or below that line. On the effort diagram, for instance, for a 100,000 line project, the source lines of code per personmonth range from about 10,000 for the most efficient producer to less than 100 for the least efficient producer. Evidently, many factors other than size affect the software production rate.

One of these additional factors is the length of development time allowed in the initial project plan. As Figure 2.2 shows, effort in personmonths falls off rapidly as the planned development time is increased. The line is not straight, indicating that the relationship is nonlinear. The Impossible Region on this figure simply means that no

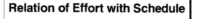

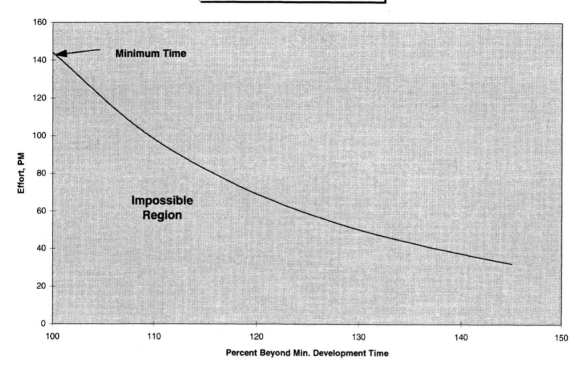

Figure 2.2   The fact that the line is curved demonstrates the nonlinear nature of the relationship between two of the management numbers: effort and (planned) development time.

organization reporting to our database has accomplished a comparable project in this short a development time.

At the time a project is planned, a manager can reduce effort (or the equivalent personmonths, manpower, staff, or cost) quite substantially by allowing a development period somewhat longer than the bare minimum.

The fact that a project team cannot complete software on too tight of a schedule is no great surprise. Organizations have demonstrated this proposition regularly over the past 40 years. Even on a tight but possible schedule, people get tired and frazzled, bite each other, make more mistakes, and spend more time correcting them. These facts of life are reflected in Figure 2.2.

Another factor in addition to size that causes the data points to spread vertically is the difference between software application types, as shown on Figure 2.3. It appears that real-time systems take longer to build at a given system size than engineering systems or information (or business) systems. The common-sense reason is that real-time

Schedule Behavior

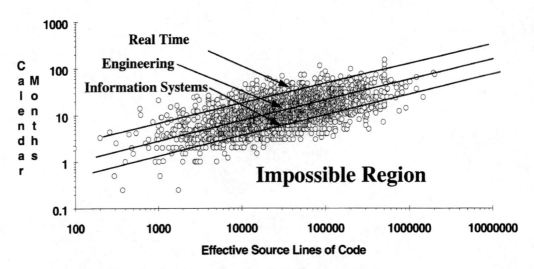

Figure 2.3 The separate mean lines for three application types are an indication that their production rates are different.

systems are more difficult. They are more difficult because they are more complex, and a complex, difficult application takes more schedule time. We could present a similar figure showing that they take more staff and effort.

On this figure, the Impossible Region shows up again. It is the zone of very short development times that contains no data points. In other words, no one has reported completing a system in this time frame, that is, less than 100 percent of the minimum development time.

The Software Relationship

With all the data points represented on Figure 2.1, we developed the mathematical relationship among the size of the software product, the effort, and the schedule. Since the diagrams show that this relationship is nonlinear, we expected it to look something like this:

Quantity of software produced equals

Some measure of the production rate, times

Effort raised to some power, times

Schedule duration raised to some power

(You can look at the actual equation in the footnote.* Shield your eyes—not everyone can stand the sight of fractional exponents.)

Determining Process Productivity

The production rate, shoes per personweek, might also be called "productivity." In the case of software development, however, the software equation represents, not the productivity of an individual shoemaker, er . . . programmer, but the ability of an entire project organization to carry out the software process from the determination of requirements, through specification writing, design, coding, and testing to delivery to the user. The software equation covers the entire project process because the management numbers from which it was derived covered the entire project. Therefore, we term this software production rate *process productivity.*

The question, then, is how to find a management number representing process productivity. Well, one could guess at it! Or, more austerely, one could gather a group of managers in a conference room and have them assess on a scale of one to fifty the

---

*Quantity of product (in source lines of code) equals

Process productivity $\times$ (Effort in personyears/Skills factor)$^{1/3}$ $\times$ (Development time in years)$^{4/3}$

We call this relationship the software equation. It was developed in the mid-1970s from production data recorded on a dozen large projects. In the 20 years since its development, we have verified it with data from more than 4,000 projects. It has also been used successfully by hundreds of software organizations to project schedules and effort. The estimated schedule has typically been within plus or minus 10 percent of the eventual actual schedule. The variance of estimated effort has been somewhat greater, but generally less than 20 percent. The software equation has stood the test of time.

Note: The effort/skills factor raised to the one-third power might also be expressed as the cube root of effort. (The skills factor reduces the weight accorded to effort and, in effect, increases the significance of development time as project size increases and the work becomes more complicated.) The cube root is a very small number, of course, indicating that the amount of effort (or manpower) plays a relatively small role compared to development time in the execution of a software project. What this means in practice is that a manager can throw a veritable horde of people at a project without getting the work done much sooner than the appropriate number of people would.

This cube-root relationship is a mathematical expression of what Fred Brooks called his "outrageously oversimplified" law: "Adding manpower to a late software project makes it later."[2]

Further note. Raising schedule time to the one and one-third power gives it a much greater weight in software development matters than effort, a fact shown graphically in Figure 2.2. Moreover, the fact that effort and schedule both appear in the software equation means that they affect one another. They are not independent of each other. They have to be planned together.

degree to which each of 15 to 20 characteristics was present in that group of wild people out there called a project team.

Fortunately, there is another approach. It is called "calibration." In engineering circles it is very respectable. For past projects, an organization has data for three of the four numbers in the software equation: quantity, effort, and schedule time. With this data, it runs the software equation backwards, so to speak.*

Calibration gives you a nice solid number for process productivity, compared with the soft number you get from an assessment approach. In assessment, someone first has to define the 15 or 20 characteristics so clearly that each of a group of disparate assessors has the same characteristic in mind. Second, all the assessors must be familiar with the organization being evaluated. Moreover, they must be familiar in some depth. People who know enough about 15 or 20 characteristics to evaluate them accurately don't grow on trees. And if, instead of using fine words like "assessment" or "evaluation," we call it "judgment," then we suspect it might be fallible. We all know people with poor judgment!

Before you get carried away contemplating the magnificence of calibration, it does carry two pieces of baggage. The first is that your organization has to have past project data and the management numbers, at least, have to be accessible, not buried in tons of unorganized old records. The accuracy of estimates depends upon the quality of metrics collected. Getting good quality metrics rests upon organizational discipline—and you know who is responsible for that! It would be nice, too, if the data were fairly consistent from one project to another. If everyone is marching to a different drummer, the management numbers from different projects won't mean the same thing. Consequently, what they might mean on the next project is uncertain.

The second is that your software organization be able to repeat its performance from one project to the next. Estimating is necessarily based on doing a familiar type of work according to an established process. If its performance is not repeatable, if its software process is not reasonably stable, it will naturally be unable to project what it can accomplish on the next project. Level 2 of the Software Engineering Institute's Capability Maturity Model is labeled "the repeatable process." About three quarters of the organizations surveyed fall below this level. For organizations at Level 1, their first step has to be to nail down the process they are using, however short of a good process it may be, so they can at least repeat their level of performance on the next project. After all, process productivity, obtained by calibration, is a reflection of the past. It is a hope that past performance can be repeated the next time. Of course, and here we are letting you in on a big secret, no estimating method can project the performance of an organization that works differently every time out of the box.

The range of process productivity numbers obtained in this way is simply enormous. Without going into detail as to what those numbers are—or how we represent

---

*Process productivity = Quantity of product (in source lines of code) ÷
(Effort in personyears/Skills factor)$^{1/3}$ × (Development time in years)$^{4/3}$

them for easy use by means of index numbers, let us merely say that the highest number yet encountered and the number at the low end differ by a factor of 2200. Individual programmers seldom differ by a factor of more than 10 to 1. It is easy to misjudge where you are on a scale of this length. Not so incidentally, the great differences in process productivity give all but the handful of organizations near the top end an incentive to improve and a notion of how far they might conceivably go. Even at the top end, however, process productivity has been increasing during the several decades that we have been watching it.

In this chapter, we have shown that you can assign a hard number to your software organization's process productivity. To use it for estimating purposes, you need a number for the quantity of software the next project is to produce. This is the subject of the next chapter.

> *Good intelligence diminishes surprise, but even the best cannot possibly prevent it altogether. Human behavior is not, and probably never will be, fully predictable.*
>
> ***Christopher Andrew***[3]

[1] P.F. Drucker, "The Information Executives Truly Need," *Harvard Business Rev.,* Jan.–Feb. 1995, pp. 54–62.

[2] F.P. Brooks, Jr., *The Mythical Man-Month: Essays in Software Engineering,* Addison-Wesley Publishing Co., Reading, Mass., 1975.

[3] C. Andrew, *For the President's Eyes Only: Secret Intelligence and the American Presidency from Washington to Bush,* Harper Collins Publishers, New York, 1995.

Chapter 3

The Key Estimate: Size

Only in software do people cling to the illusion that it's OK to come up with estimates of the future, even though you've never measured anything in the past.

Tom DeMarco [1]

What we would really like to do is estimate the quantity of work to be done on a software project. The quantity of work, if we could establish it, would be a very good indicator of the amount of effort and time needed to do the work. We would be well on the way to a project plan and estimate. But what is *quantity of work?*

In physics, work is defined as the product of a force (being applied against resistance) over a distance. In software development, we might say, comparably, that work is the product of (largely human) force applied over time, that is:

$$\text{Work} = \text{Number of People} \times \text{Years}$$

This relationship, if we add a process productivity term, looks similar to the software equation of the previous chapter. Work has now been substituted for *quantity of software*. Software, of course, is the work product. Apparently we need a way to estimate the quantity of software the project is to produce.

Measures for Quantity

The most common measure of the quantity of software is source lines of code. It is the principal measure that software people have used to quantify completed projects. At the point of planning a project, however, we cannot measure it, for the software does not yet exist. We can only estimate what it will eventually be.

Some software people are dubious about using source lines of code as the sole measure of all the work making up a software project—requirements, specifications, architecture, design, coding, testing, and documentation. Only coding, they say, is properly measured by source lines of code. To the contrary, we say: The code is the ultimate product that goes to the users' computers. It incorporates all the work that led up to it.

Perhaps a personal computer user can code without formally establishing requirements, design, and so forth, but software produced on a business basis is the functional expression of all the steps of the software life cycle.

Other people say that *function points,* which measure the functionality of software, are a better indicator of what a project has produced. This technique counts the number of *functions,* that is, inputs, outputs, inquiries, master files, and interfaces. As soon as the system architecture is established, a software architect or designer can get a good count of the number of functions.

People have used still other functional representations: number of subsystems, programs, entities, modules, objects, or components. As object-oriented technology becomes more widespread and as the reuse of components becomes more common, we may expect to see functionality represented in terms of objects or components more often.

At a fundamental level, however, these are all size units. They are all representations at differing levels of abstractions of size, that is, quantity of code. A subsystem, for instance, in our experience ranges from 4,000 to 12,000 source lines of code. Objects range from 700 to 1,200; modules, from 100 to 500; function points, from 20 to 400. Those are substantial spreads, but in any one organization, using consistent procedures, the range is much narrower. In short, if you estimate in objects, components, modules, etc., you can develop a *gearing factor* from your own data to convert your estimate to source lines of code.

People Estimate Size

We don't know of any way to obtain size by "calibration." People have to do it. After making a little fun of people's judgment in the last chapter, we come to this point a bit chastened. Still, chastened or not, we know that human judgment is fallible. People need all the help they can get in estimating size.

One way of strengthening their judgment is to stuff their heads with information about their organization's past experience. In other words, keep size data on your past projects; keep it in an easily accessible form, such as a database accessible from personal computers.

Another way to improve judgment is to use the best heads you have for size estimating—experienced managers, software architects, senior designers.

Use more than one head, probably three or four. The over-optimistic judgments of one person will offset the over-pessimistic judgments of another. That is why we have boards of directors and executive committees, instead of just single executives.

Give the estimating group time to learn something about the forthcoming project. The more they know about the proposed software, the more accurately they can forecast its size.

Do not expect them to pinpoint a size, such as 65,702 source lines of code. At the same time, look suspiciously upon a round number, such as 50,000 lines. Ask them to come up with a range: the minimum size is 55,000; the most likely size is 66,000; the maximum size is 79,000.

This is the Delphi technique popularized decades ago by PERT planning. From this three-point estimate, one can calculate the expected size and its standard deviation, as shown in Figure 3.1.* The standard deviation is a statistical way of formally expressing the uncertainty of an estimate. This uncertainty can be carried all the way through the estimating procedure to provide an indication of the degree of risk associated with the ultimate estimates of effort and time. Risk management starts at this point.

When a hopeful few first broach the concept of a project—perhaps to keep California from sliding into the Pacific Ocean—they know little about the architecture of the software that may be involved. At this point, if called on to estimate the effort and time, the estimators can only propose a very wide spread between the minimum size and the maximum size. They are picking an expected value within a "ballpark."

Later, when the scope of the proposal has been narrowed to the software that will calculate the stresses on the wall in front of the governor's beach cottage, the estimators have a much firmer grasp of the nature of this software. They can reduce the range between their minimum and maximum estimates.

Thus, as requirements become more precisely defined, as feasibility is established, and as architecture is firmed up, the knowledge available to estimators increases. Their estimate of size can become firmer.

Manpower Buildup Rate

Manpower buildup refers to the rate at which people are applied to a project during the period in which the staff curve is rising.† Of course, management might unwisely assign people to a new project at some arbitrary rate. If management heeds signals from

---

*Expected size = (Minimum size + 4 × Most likely size + Maximum size)/6

Choose the minimum size so that only a few outliers—less than one percent—would be smaller. Similarly, choose the maximum size so that less than one percent would be larger.

Standard deviation = (Maximum − Minimum)/6

†We introduce the manpower buildup rate at this point because it is one of the inputs to the estimation process discussed in the next chapter. Mathematically, the software equation is one equation with two unknowns, effort and time. To solve for both effort and time, we need a second equation, and the one for manpower buildup serves this purpose:

Manpower buildup is proportional to $(\text{Effort/Development time})^3$

Size Estimating Approach

- **The weighted averaging technique shifts the expected value in skewed size distributions in the direction of long tail**

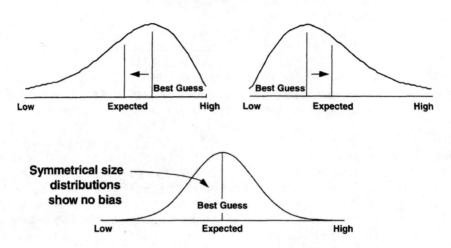

The shape of the size distribution indicates the degree of risk

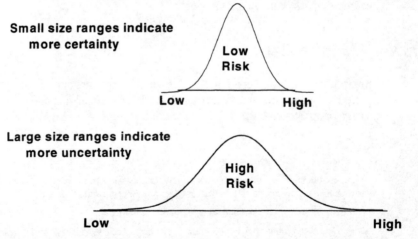

Figure 3.1   Three-point estimates are a statistical method of turning low, high, and most-likely estimates into an expected value for use in further analysis. A small standard deviation represents low risk; a large standard deviation means more uncertainty about the estimated number, which translates into high risk.

the project, however, it will supply people at the rate necessary to staff tasks as they are broken out by the architects and senior designers. Also, some tasks cannot be commenced until information from a previous task has been obtained. That is why the staffing curve does not rise vertically at the moment of project beginning.

Manpower buildup, like process productivity, is a metric obtained by calibration from past project data. So long as an organization is doing much the same kind of applications with the same process, people, and management, the manpower buildup rate is likely to remain the same. Management has few levers with which to speed it up. Of course, it could slow the rate down by the simple expedient of failing to assign people when tasks are ready. Usually the pressure of meeting schedule causes management to assign people, if possible, to keep up with the tasks as they become available.

Even today, industry surveys indicate that only about 25 percent of application development organizations have a formal metrics program.[2]

Ed Yourdon

[1] S. Brady and T. DeMarco, "Management-Aided Software Engineering," *IEEE Software,* vol. 11, no. 6, Nov. 1994, pp. 25–32.

[2] E. Yourdon, "Software Metrics," Application Development Strategies, Nov. 1994.

Chapter 4

Estimating Schedule and Effort

All too many consultants, when asked "What is two and two?" respond, "What did you have in mind?"

Norman Augustine[1]

The estimate of software size and the calibrated values of process productivity and manpower buildup are the principal inputs to the software estimation process, diagrammed in Figure 4.1. We could, of course, put in the expected values of these numbers, solve the software equation and the manpower buildup equation, and obtain single values for effort and schedule. These single values, however, would represent only one of many possible plans under which we could carry out the project. In fact, these single values would give us only a 50-percent probability of completing the project within the limits they set.

Moreover, single values are not true to how software people experience life in the trenches. In the real world, the management numbers associated with the development of software are "uncertain," to use a rather mild term. Not only are they uncertain, they are often plain wrong. As a result, projects overrun their schedules, staff allocations, and budgets. A product with a grievous number of defects is delivered. Senior managers find it necessary to cancel quite a few projects altogether.

What the software industry needs is fairly obvious when you stop to think about it: an estimation methodology that can arrive at reasonably accurate estimates; a way to transform uncertainties in the estimating inputs into probabilities of achieving the output numbers; a way of taking the constraints under which an organization works into account in making estimates; and a method of spreading overall estimates of staff, effort, cost, and defect detection over the time period of the main build.

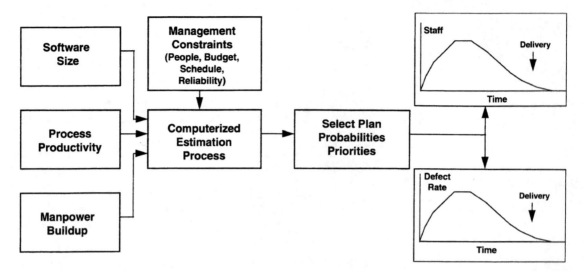

Figure 4.1 From size, process productivity, and manpower buildup rate, estimators can project effort, schedule, and defects. Moreover, they can see the effects of management constraints—number of people, maximum budget, desired schedule, needed reliability—on the plan.

Achieve Reasonably Accurate Estimates

Technically, it may not be possible to project completely accurate estimates of cost, effort, schedule, and the like, but it is possible to forecast reasonably accurate estimates. We know it is possible because many organizations are doing it. For example, we analyzed 664 projects completed between 1987 and 1991. Their average size was 78,215 source lines of code; their average schedule was 11.56 months; their average effort was 113.98 personmonths.

More than half finished practically on their estimates. Specifically, 53 percent finished either on time or within one month of the planned completion date and another quarter completed within two or three months of the scheduled date.

Effort performance was equally as good, with 62 percent finishing either on budget or within 5 personmonths of the planned effort and 73 percent completing within 10 personmonths of plan.

This achievement is not characteristic of the entire software industry. Those reporting to us are making measurements and using process methods. Their record does establish that accurate estimating, often within five percent and mostly within 10 percent, is within the state of the art.

Transform Uncertainty to Probability

The size estimate, as we have seen, is uncertain. If the eventual actual size turns out to be on the low end of the estimate range, it is likely that effort and development time will also be relatively low. Similarly, if the actual size is at the high end of the estimate range, effort and time will also be relatively high. A mathematical method called simulation enables an estimator to forecast, for example, that the probability is 75 percent that the organization can complete the project in so many personmonths and so many calendar months.

The simulation method assumes that there are, say, 1,000 values of the size estimate between the minimum and the maximum values that the estimators selected. It assumes that few of these values fall near the minimum and few near the maximum. About two thirds fall near the mean, specifically, within plus and minus one standard deviation of the expected size.

Using this distribution of values, the simulation method makes 1,000 computations and gets 1,000 values of effort and time. These values, too, are distributed over a range, that is, with most near the expected mean values and a few farther out. The probability is 99 percent, for example, that the organization can complete the project within the largest values of effort and time. Similarly, lesser percentage probabilities are associated with lesser values of effort and time. At the other end of the scale, the probability is only one percent that the organization can complete the project within the values of effort and time found there.

In the preceding chapters, we assumed that process productivity and manpower buildup were single numbers. If an organization has recorded its past project data carefully, our assumption is almost true. If the metrics have been poorly defined and their collection weakly disciplined, the values of process productivity and manpower buildup, too, will be spread over a range.

Worse yet, if there are no records of past projects with which to calibrate these metrics, then they, too, have to be estimated. Estimators must then define characteristics and evaluate the degree to which they are present—a process which we made some fun of earlier on. In the absence of metrics, however, that is the only option. In the outcome, of course, the uncertainty of values arrived at in this way will be great. Depending on the circumstances, the simulation computation has to use a range of values for these two inputs with a corresponding effect on the output values of effort and time.

Circumstances Constrain Estimates

Management operates in a world constrained by customers' needs and resource limitations, specifically:

- Customers or users may want the software product by a date that fits some larger schedule they are trying to meet.

- Someone (Congress, a contracting officer, the capital budget committee) may have ordained a budget that looks pretty firm.
- You may need to have a minimum number of people on the project staff in order to provide the different skills needed and to assure continuity through vacations, illness, and resignations.
- There may be a maximum number of people that you can allocate to a project, because that is all the people you have, or that is all the space you have to house them.
- The customer or user may specify a mean time to defect at the time of delivery. Or, in the absence of a specified mean time to defect, the nature of the function the software is to perform may tacitly set a reliability goal. See Chapter 5.

Of course, these constraints cannot be entirely arbitrary. They have to be within the limits of what is possible—what your organization can achieve.

For each one of these constraints, you would like to be able to input three numbers to the estimation process: (1) its numerical value, for example, 34.00 schedule months; (2) the desired probability of achieving the value, for example, 75 percent; (3) the weight to be assigned to each constraint, relative to the others.

Process the Estimate by Computer

At this point, you have two exponential equations, uncertain inputs to be calculated by simulation, and a batch of constraints with desired probabilities and priorities. As you might suspect, you want to find a plan that meets all these conditions. Moreover, you want to be able to change this plan to see if some other combination better suits the intangibles that you have kept in the back of your mind.

Doing all this will wear down your pencil, you say? It certainly would. Moreover, it would take you a couple of months. Fortunately, we now live in the computer age. Computers, even inexpensive personal or laptop computers, love to do work like this. To them, exponentiation, statistical computations, linear programming, diagram drawing, and the other skills this estimation process uses are fun! All you have to do is apply your knowledge of the general situation in which you are operating to the computer's output.*

---

*In modern technology, expounding the concept is usually only the beginning of the work to be done. For example, the concept that high-level source code is a better way to write software than machine code or assembly instructions is simple. Before it could be used, however, someone had to develop a source language, such as Fortran or COBOL, and interpreters and compilers to translate it into machine code.

Similarly, software estimating methods that utilize thousands of computations involving exponential equations, constraints, uncertainty, and risk, and thousands of additional computations to output curves and their corresponding tables, are beyond the range of an unaided human being.

What the computer initially gives you is the solution that comes closest to meeting all the conditions you lay down. Specifically, it shows you the development time, effort, cost, peak staff, and mean time to defect; for each output, it lists the calculated probability of achieving that number next to the probability that you set. The computer draws curves and diagrams that graphically show these results.

The odds are that you initially set some constraints that your organization can't achieve at your current process productivity level or manpower buildup rate. For instance, you may have set a probability constraint of 75 percent on the development time you listed. That is, you wanted a 75-percent probability of meeting a development time of 34 months. The computation comes back with 21 percent. In other words, you are not likely to complete the job on your original terms.

No problem. You change some of the terms. Perhaps you extend the schedule to 35 months. You can make this change by entering the new number in a dialogue box or by moving a "handle" on the staff curve a little to the right. The output numbers or the curve immediately change to show you the effect of your change. You can quickly run through a series of "what if" possibilities.

Project Estimates over Main Build

So far, we have been thinking in terms of length of schedule and overall effort (staff and cost). For operational planning and control purposes, managers also need to spread these estimates over the period of development. Experience shows that these management numbers distribute themselves along a Rayleigh curve, similar to the two curves drawn at the right side of Figure 4.1. The slope of the rising edge of the curve depends on the manpower buildup rate.

Management numbers projected in this way include staff headcount (that is, number of people required each week or month), cost per month, and defect rate. The area under the curve is proportional to the effort (personmonths).

Estimation vs. Bidding

Estimation is the technical process of going from what is known about a project before formal work starts to the expected size, range of that size, schedule, effort, defect rate (or mean time to defect) and the probability of meeting those goals. Effective estimation requires some means of knowing what process productivity and manpower buildup will be.

In our case, a personal computer performs these tasks under the control of software estimating tools developed under Putnam's supervision[2]. In addition, half a dozen companies provide tools based on the COCOMO model, first published by Barry Boehm in 1981[3]. Still other companies provide tools based on proprietary models[4].

Bidding is the management process of deciding what numbers are necessary to win a piece of business—to satisfy a customer or gain a user. The bid may differ from the best estimate. With computer assistance, the best estimate may be quickly modified to meet necessary bid circumstances. Moreover, the effect of bid-induced changes may be noted. For instance, the probability of successful completion at the proposed bid values of schedule and effort may fall to 25 percent. That may be necessary for very good reasons, unpleasant as it is to contemplate. But you know what you're in for. You have time to plot a strategy.

> *This is the time when grown men gather in a room in each company and spend the time not trying to decide what the cost would really be, but trying to guess what the grown men in the other rooms are going to guess.*
>
> *Norman Augustine*[1]

[1] N.R. Augustine, *Augustine's Laws,* Penguin Books, New York, 1983.

[2] L.H. Putnam and W. Myers, *Measures for Excellence: Reliable Software On Time, Within Budget,* Yourdon Press, Prentice-Hall, Englewood Cliffs, N.J., 1992.

[3] B.W. Boehm, *Software Engineering Economics,* Prentice-Hall, Englewood Cliffs, N.J., 1981.

[4] A.E. Giles and D. Barney, "Metrics Tools: Software Cost Estimation," *CrossTalk,* June 1995, pp. 7–10.

Chapter 5

Forecasting Defects

The truth, ironically first discovered some years ago by an American, W. Edwards Deming, and exported to Japan when American industrialists wouldn't listen to him, is that higher quality begets not increased cost but reduced cost. This is the miracle of productivity and quality.

Norman Augustine[1]

The number of defects incurred in developing software can be forecast. The forecast takes the form of Figure 5.1. Points on the curve at each time point are the defect rate (such as defects per month). The defect rate starts out small when few people are working on the project, increases to a peak when many people are at work, and declines as the number of people tails off. The pattern is the same Rayleigh curve that the number of staff follows.

The area under the curve is proportional to the total number of defects. The area under the curve to the right of the time of delivery (line labeled **Dev. Time**) is the number of defects delivered to the user. The reciprocal of the defect rate is the mean time to defect. For example, a defect rate of 30 defects per month corresponds to a mean time to defect of 1/30 month, or one day. Many consider this metric to be more helpful than the defect rate because it is more directly related to users' needs.

The defect rate is a useful metric during development, because developers make errors during specification writing, architectural design, detailed design, coding, and unit testing. Throughout this period, there is no operating software to run for a mean time to defect. Mean time to defect becomes a useful metric only in system testing and later, when there is a system to operate.

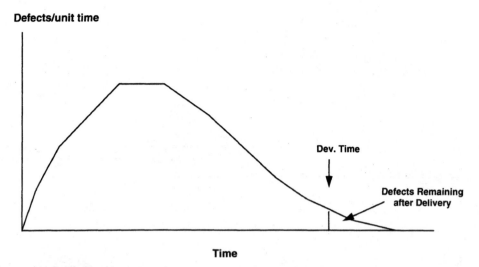

Figure 5.1   Project planners project defects per month as a Rayleigh curve. The area under the curve is proportional to the total number of defects. The small area following the delivery point (line labeled Dev. Time) represents the number of defects remaining in the product at the time of delivery.

Defect Drivers

People commit errors. In software development, people are the principal factor. Therefore, as the staff level of a project rises (along the leading edge of the Rayleigh curve), the number of errors also rises. In fact, the rise in errors is nonlinear. The increase in the quantity of interactions between people as the number of people rises is one of the factors responsible for the nonlinear rate of increase.

A second defect driver is time pressure. As time pressure builds, people make more errors. In terms of software development, if you push the rate of staff buildup or shorten the development period, the increase in time pressure causes the error rate to rise.

A third defect driver is the size of the software product. As we saw in Figure 2.1, the number of errors is proportional to the source lines of code.

A fourth defect driver is process productivity. Our data show that increasing process productivity decreases the number of defects in a nonlinear fashion. This data surprises some people, who figure that if developers take more care to avoid errors, that will reduce the volume of work they turn out. But process productivity encompasses more than an individual working carefully. It reflects all the factors impacting productivity: methods, tools, techniques, people skills and training, and management capability. One of the effects of improving these factors is to reduce errors. Moreover, if developers commit fewer errors early in the life cycle, they spend less time and resources correcting them late in the cycle.

In general, the defect-rate curve follows the same pattern as the staff curve, but time pressure and process productivity influence its exact shape. Given data on past projects, we derived a defect forecasting algorithm. It forecasts a Rayleigh curve of defect rate, similar to Figure 5.1. After system test gets under way, it forecasts a curve for mean time to defect. These projections are based on industry-wide data. Your own experience probably differs somewhat from this average. You need the capability to fine tune the defect-rate curve to reflect your own experience.

Tuning the Defect Projection

In the case of completed projects, an organization can, using the industry-based algorithms, project a defect-rate curve from its past data on schedule, effort, and process productivity. Then it can, in effect, pencil in its own defect-rate curve of actual past data. The difference between the two curves provides the information with which to fine tune the defect-rate curve of its next project.

In practice, fine tuning can be simplified to two steps: (1) Count the number of defects encountered between the beginning of system test and delivery (on three to five past projects); (2) Find out from a typical user, or several users, the average number of days the software was able to operate before encountering a fault during the first month of operation. A fine-tuning algorithm then adjusts the defect-rate forecast of the project coming up.

Reduce Errors

"All this talk of projecting defect rates makes me feel that we are missing the point," an executive told us. "Why not get rid of the errors in the first place?"

Amen. Of course we should. One way to whip up interest in avoiding errors is to count them as they are found and compare that number with what you expected to find—the projected fine-tuned curve. If the two are going along in tandem, at least the project is on the expected track. If the defect rate is exceeding the forecast, the forecast may be wrong, but chances are the fault lies in the way people are executing the project. Look for the problem. If the defect rate is less than the forecast, the forecast may be wrong, but, more likely, the project is going well. See if you can find out why and encourage other teams to follow the good example.

It is possible to reduce the number of errors committed by the use of techniques known as *formal methods* or *cleanroom engineering*. Unfortunately, using these techniques is not easy. Training developers to use them is expensive and time consuming. So far, they have not been widely used, but you might ask one of your best technical people to keep an eye on them. At some point your organization might be ready to use them.

A technique of several decades standing is software inspection, recently detailed in a book of the same name by Tom Gilb and Dorothy Graham[2]. The general idea is to find errors close to the time at which people commit them. A developer and a group of his or her immediate associates look for them in requirements, specification, design, or code while the work is still fresh in their minds. That is the first step in the inspection process.

When they find an error, the developer who made it can fix it quickly and correctly, that is, without introducing additional errors. In contrast, when an organization makes little effort to find errors until test, finding the error (by now a fault) costs more. Worse, the cause of a fault in test is usually not obvious. The original cause may lie two or three stages back, in design or specifications. The developer responsible for that section of the project may no longer be readily available. Even if the developer is nearby, it is now months later, and his or her memory of what was done has dimmed. Also, the likelihood of introducing further errors in the course of fixing the first one is greater.

If an organization has largely deferred finding and fixing defects until test, its defect-rate curve will bulge at that point. Later, if it begins early inspections, the defect-rate curve will move to earlier points in the life cycle. The organization may find it necessary to make an allowance for this shift in the curve to earlier time. It is likely, however, that the inspection process will grow gradually over a time span covering several project cycles. The shift in the projections between successive projects will be small.

Another approach that promises to reduce the incidence of defects is reuse of software that has already been freed of defects—or almost freed. Nothing is perfect in the imperfect software world. We may reuse algorithms, modules, objects, subsystems, designs, specifications, and even requirements or portions of them. Of course, there are problems in reusing software components. If it were easy, we would already be doing it on a larger scale than is now the case.

The mechanics of actually inventorying and reusing software components lie in the province of software technologists. Providing the needed investment, policies and procedures, and staff training to implement reuse requires the participation of management.

The Ultimate Goal: Quality

"Quality" is in the eye of the beholder, the poet said, much later in life when "beauty" had worn thin. Just so, and in software, quality is in the eye of the user, later in the life cycle.

Quality is one of the three ultimate arbiters of a product's success, along with cost and getting to market at the appropriate time. Quality is important, whether the product sells at a price to a worldwide market or is distributed to departments within the same company.

The process of determining users' requirements and then meeting them on time and within cost is the first step to quality. The further process of observing the software's operation in the users' environment in order to make further progress toward meeting their needs, either in additional releases of the product or enhancement during so-called maintenance, is equally important.

One aspect of quality is reliability. Technically speaking, reliability refers to the probability that a software product can operate without failure in a specified environment for a specified time. It is commonly measured by the metric, mean time to defect. As we have seen, mean time to defect is the reciprocal of the defect rate. Therefore, detecting and correcting defects as development transpires is a first step to reliability, which is, in turn, an important step toward quality.

> *Successful management of any process requires planning, measurement, and control. In programming development, these requirements translate into defining the programming process in terms of a series of operations, each operation having its own exit criteria. Next there must be some means of measuring completeness of the product at any point of its development by inspections or testing. And finally, the measured data must be used for controlling the process.*
>
> ***Michael E. Fagan***[3]

[1] N.R. Augustine, *Augustine's Laws,* Penguin Books, New York, 1983.

[2] T. Gilb and D. Graham, *Software Inspection,* Addison-Wesley Publishing Co., Reading, Mass., 1993.

[3] M.E. Fagan, "Design and Code Inspections to Reduce Errors in Program Development," *IBM Systems J.,* Vol. 15, No. 1, 1976, pp. 219–248.

Chapter 6

Managers Control Schedule— and Influence Results Thereby

There is a limit to how many man-months of effort can be squeezed into a given elapsed time, and the edge of the Impossible Region marks that limit.

Tom DeMarco[1]

Being a manager empowers one to give orders, doesn't it? And hence, to set project schedules. Yes, but. . . . Under the influence of customer hopes, apparent market windows, or the need to bring in revenue, some managers do set down what later turn out to be unrealistic schedules. Some managers feel that setting tight schedules keeps the troops on their toes. Yes, but—overly tight schedules also carry costs of their own. The most obvious one is when the schedule is so tight that the development time planned is down in the Impossible Region. The troops may start out with high morale, but impossibility has a way of dampening their spirits.

It is generally fairly high-level managers and executives who finally determine project schedules and budgets. It follows that, while engineering-level people may work out the plans, software projects will be executed more successfully if executives understand the limitations under which the projects operate.

How Much Time Pressure?

We visualize these planning relationships in Figure 6.1. At the point in time at which we plan effort and schedule, we have already estimated two management numbers: size (source lines of code) and process productivity. Size-divided-by-process-productivity appears as a straight line on a log-log diagram of effort vs. schedule time.

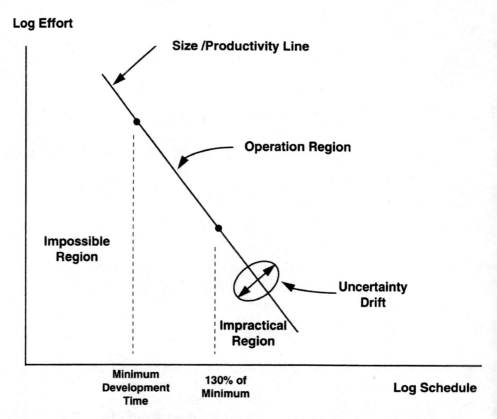

Figure 6.1   Between the Impossible Region and the Impractical Region, software developers can choose an effort-development time pair in the Operating Region. Within this region they can reduce effort, cost, (and defects) by planning a little longer schedule.

We know there is a minimum development time, marked by the left-hand dot. Basically, this dot location is derived from a large database of past projects. No organization of similar productivity has ever completed a comparable project in less time. To the left of this point lies the Impossible Region.

Similarly, we know there is a practical maximum development time, marked by the right-hand dot. This point is less firmly located than the minimum time, but experience indicates that 130 percent of the minimum development time is a reasonable location for it. Beyond that point, effort (staff) may drop below the level that supplies all needed skills to the project and allows for vacations, unexpected illness, or terminations. A schedule longer than 130 percent may exacerbate executive time-pressured dyspepsia, too.

Between these two dots lies the feasible Operating Region. Along this short length of line, estimators can select a combination of effort and development time that their organization can accomplish. Such a selection, however, is not a single, certain number. To the extent that we are uncertain of the true size and process productivity, the size-divided-by-process-productivity line may shift, as shown by the arrows. The line, as drawn in Figure 6.1, is the "expected" line, that is, there is a 50-percent probability that the "true" line lies to the left, but also a 50-percent probability that it lies to the right.

If the size is greater than the "expected" value, the line moves to the right. Then both effort and development time increase. Or, if process productivity is less than the "expected" value, the line also moves to the right. Conversely, if the size is less than expected or the process productivity is greater, the line moves to the left.

The probability is high that the "true" line lies near the "expected" position where we have drawn it. The probability is low that the line lies farther out, either to the right or left. If the line is far out, both effort and time will be substantially affected. These uncertainties can be taken into account in calculating effort and time by the statistical methods referred to in Chapter 4.

Whatever these uncertainties may be in a specific case, the estimator has many effort-time pairs between the minimum development time and the Impractical Region from which to choose. This choice has an effect on the length of schedule and the amount of effort needed to complete the project. Of course, effort is proportional to number of staff and cost.

Glancing at Figure 6.1, it is evident that, by lengthening the planned development time, the estimator can count on greatly reduced effort. Conversely, by shortening the planned development time, the estimator can expect to reap higher costs. We have often observed at planning time that various factions press for a tighter schedule. Marketing wants to meet some target date it believes the customer needs. Or the tight schedule may be the outcome of something as simple as round numbers: we want to do it in a year, when a reasonable schedule would be 14.6 months. Yet a year later no one seems much excited because the schedule has indeed slipped several months.

They would be more concerned if they realized the cost implications. First, planning to do the project in 12 months shoves the effort and cost up higher than the effort and cost of the 14.6-month schedule would be. Second, when the project misses the unreasonable delivery date, the cost of extending the schedule two or three months adds to that high figure.

As we noted in Chapter 5, effort and time pressure also drive the rate of defect occurrence. Thus, if we lengthen development time, reducing time pressure and effort, we also reduce the number of errors developers commit. The project spends less time in inspection and test finding and correcting defects. The defects remaining at delivery are fewer. The customer receives a more reliable product.

Figure 6.2 illustrates six plans for executing a typical information systems project of 75,000 source lines of code. The organization has average process productivity (of those reporting data to us). The lowest line depicts the most efficient plan—six people at a cost of $416,000—albeit the one with the longest development time (13.6 months). As we shorten the schedule, the number of staff increases, as detailed in Table 6.1.

Different Staffing Plans

Staffing

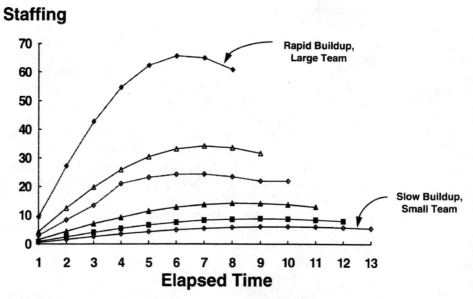

Figure 6.2 The six lines show the peak staff-development time relationship between six plans to accomplish the same project—a 75,000-line information system at average process productivity. The lowest line calls for six people, but takes the longest time. Reading up, the plans take 9, 14, 24, 33, and 66 people, as detailed in Table 6.1.

Table 6.1 Typical information systems project of 75,000 source lines of code accomplished at average process productivity. As the schedule is progressively reduced, rate of staff buildup increases, peak staff increases, cost increases, and mean time to defect declines.

Staff buildup	Peak staff	Schedule (months)	Cost ($)	MTTD (days)
Slow	6	13.6	416,000	4.8
Moderately slow	9	12.3	623,000	3.2
Moderate	14	11.3	875,000	2.1
Rapid	24	10.2	1,300,000	1.2
Very rapid	33	9.5	1,700,000	0.9
Extremely rapid	66	8.3	3,000,000	0.4

How Big? How Complex?

The size of the proposed product and complexity of the work to be done naturally affect the length of schedule and the amount of effort, as we showed in Figure 2.3. They also affect the number of errors. Development time, effort, and defects increase with size (or functionality, however measured). Real-time systems at a given size, because they are more complex, take more time and effort and incur more errors than information systems.

There is not much that the software engineers on the project can do about either size or complexity. Usually, to them, size and complexity are givens. The marketplace, the external customer, or the internal user have indicated what they want. Software marketing and management have acquiesced or sometimes negotiated a bit. If anything is to be done—or can be done—it is clearly in the province of management to initiate it.

When estimators turn requirements into schedule, effort, and defect figures, they sometimes find that these figures considerably exceed the customer's schedule, budget, and reliability hopes. You, as an executive, then face three choices.

(1) You may accede to the customer's requirements, schedule, budget, and mean time to failure, find that they are in or near the Impossible Region, and hope for the best. Doing this occasionally—buying in—may be defended. Doing it consistently . . . well, fill in your own scenario.

(2) If you don't like that scenario, you can try to negotiate a better schedule and price. Here, the kind of analysis that Figure 6.1 represents gives you an arsenal of talking points. With a longer development time, the number of errors declines and delivered reliability improves. The probability of meeting the delivery date improves.

(3) You can try to negotiate down the proposed functionality, thus reducing size and in some cases, complexity. Then, you may be able to meet the user's schedule, effort, and reliability targets. The probability of meeting them improves.

How Efficient?

The trade-offs of time for reduced effort and improved reliability and of functionality for shortened schedule operate on the time scale of a project. On a longer time scale, stretching over years, management can take actions that lead to greatly improved process productivity, a subject to which we return in Chapter 9. In the meantime, we just note that getting more efficient—by which we mean improving process productivity—gives us the best of all possible worlds. Getting more efficient is not a trade-off. To those who practice efficiency, it gives shorter schedules, less effort and cost, and fewer defects—all the outcomes we want. And that is just at the project level.

We might note parenthetically that successful projects mean profits, not losses; satisfied users, not big, bad bears on the telephone; a going software organization, not one fraying at its seams. But you know these things. We'll shut up.

Common Sense Backed by Analysis

Most of the points we have made in this chapter are common sense. What may not be common-sense evident is that the various management numbers are not independent. That is the point of this chapter: these numbers interact with each other. A little less time pressure leads to less cost and better reliability. A little less size and complexity results in a shorter schedule with fewer errors. A little more efficiency betters all the other management numbers. To paraphrase an old song: you can't have one without the others.

Also, what may not have been so obvious is the sharpness of the trade-offs. The size-divided-by-process-productivity line in Figure 6.1 sits at a steep angle: a little extension of time gives you a large reduction in effort, as given numerical life in Figure 6.2 and Table 6.1. For example, an improvement of your process productivity from a point somewhat below average to a point somewhat above average increases your organizational efficiency by a factor of seven!* This "lucky number" is not a pipe dream. About one-sixth of the organizations reporting data to us are now that far or farther above average.

To take advantage of these trade-offs, however, you need to be backed up by data. That means you have to measure what your software organization is doing, have analysts who can put it in the form you can use, and have it accessible, such as on the workstation or personal computer screen in your office. Hundreds of software organizations are already doing this[2].

If you have data on your organization's past projects readily available (on that same screen), you can compare the estimates for schedule, effort, cost, and defects of the proposed project to the actuals on similar completed projects. If your current estimate is close to what your organization has accomplished in the recent past, you can feel comfortable with it. If it is off base, someone may have put in an unrealistic figure. Further, with access to an industry-wide database, you could see how you stack up with the kind of organizations you may be competing with.

One final point. Making these trade-offs and improving process productivity are management calls. They are where you can make a difference in the way your organization does software development.

So extending delivery time will reduce total development cost up to a point.

Tom DeMarco[1]

[1] T. DeMarco, *Controlling Software Projects,* Yourdon Press, New York, 1982.

[2] L.H. Putnam and W. Myers, *Measures for Excellence: Reliable Software On Time, Within Budget,* Yourdon Press, Prentice-Hall, Englewood Cliffs, N.J., 1992.

---

* Specifically, this comparison refers to an information systems software organization improving from one standard deviation below mean process productivity to one standard deviation above mean. For engineering systems, the factor is four; for real-time systems, three.

Chapter 7

Monitoring Project Progress

There are two time-proven ways to track progress on a software project. The first is to track completed functionality . . . lines of code . . . The second is . . . found-and-fixed defects.

Robert B. Grady[1]

As we begin this chapter, we have obtained process productivity and manpower build-up by calibration and made estimates of size, development time, effort (cost and staff), and defects. Using these estimates, we have made a proposal and received a go-ahead. We now need to project these estimates over the period of development.

These projections are needed, not only by project managers for immediate project-control purposes, but also by higher levels of management with broader responsibilities. These managers are responsible for providing resources (staff, space, computer time, working capital) to enable a number of projects to follow their plans. The managers, in turn, must plan to transfer resources between projects as some wind down and others build up. They need to know the amount of staff and resources that will be available months ahead of time to gauge the organization's ability to undertake new work. Summing the projections of all an organization's projects provides this kind of information to senior managers.

Projecting Staff, Defects, and Work Accomplished

We saw in Chapter 1 that the staff projection will be in the form of a Rayleigh curve. Given estimates for process productivity, manpower buildup, size, development time, and total effort (which is the area under the Rayleigh curve), we can (on the basis of established mathematical methods) draw such a curve, as shown in Figure 7.1A. This

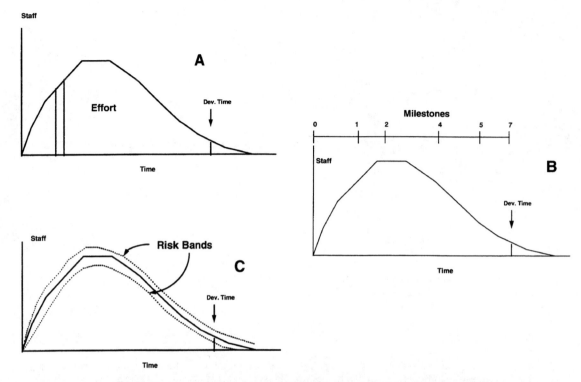

Figure 7.1   (A) Managers can project estimates of staff (or defects, or code constructed) over development time. (B) They can locate milestones on the projections, signifying that some stage of the work has been completed. (C) To take the uncertainties involved in estimates into account, they can locate risk bands (or control limits) around the line of expected values.

curve shows the number of people needed each month. This number, for each month of the project, can also be tabulated.

In Chapter 5, we saw that the defect rate follows a similar pattern. People commit errors at about the same rate as staff hours are expended. Here we are referring not just to errors in writing code, but also to errors in developing requirements, specifications, designs, and test plans. It is likely that the curve of errors committed would be in the same time span as the staff curve. However, we don't have a way of recording an error until someone finds it. If an organization is following an early-inspection policy, the curve of defects found may lag the staff curve by only a few weeks. If it waits for test to turn up faults, the curve of defects found may lag the staff curve by many months. If not caught earlier, errors eventually turn up as faults in code.

We can project a typical defect-rate curve from industry-wide data, modified by the process productivity and manpower buildup rate of the particular organization.

Because of differences in inspection policy and effectiveness, an organization can further tune the curve to fit its own way of working. In addition, once we project a defect-rate curve, we can project its reciprocal, the mean-time-to-defect curve.

The commonly used size unit is source lines of code. An organization can, if it wishes, measure in other units, such as function points, objects, or modules. These are convertible into source lines of code. Again, the Rayleigh size or code-construction curve is generally proportional to effort.

Key measurement points are called milestones. They occur at points in development time as suggested by Figure 7.1B. They represent another way to gauge progress on a project. Two sets of milestones are listed in Table 7.1. Users could employ other milestone sets.

As we saw in earlier chapters, our estimates of effort and development time are uncertain. It follows that the position of expected or mean lines in projections of Rayleigh curves will also be uncertain. We can visualize this uncertainty by means of risk bands, as shown in Figure 7.1C. The risk bands or control limits are often spaced at plus and minus one standard deviation from the expected line. The odds are then two

Table 7.1 The first column contains the milestones that were used (before DoD standard 2176A) by the U.S. Department of Defense (except the last two) and has often been employed, sometimes under other names, by other developers[2]. The second column is a set suggested by a commercial developer[3].

0	Feasibility study review	Executive concept approval
1	Preliminary design review	Scope approval
2	Critical design review	Specification approval
3	First code complete	
4	Start of system integration test	Functional capability
5	Start of user-oriented system test	
6	Initial operating capability	Fully functional
7	Full operational capability	Release
8	99-percent reliability level	
9	99.9-percent reliability level	

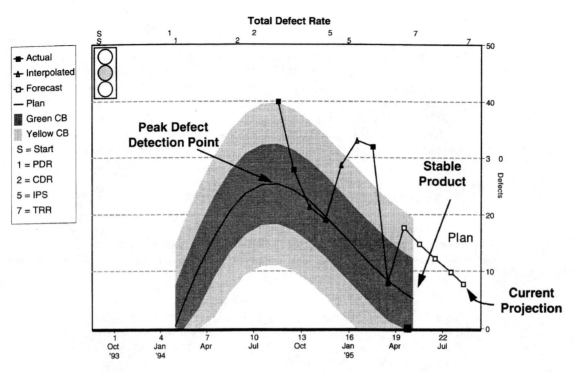

Figure 7.2 The computer-drawn version of a defect-rate curve looks like this. The milestone numbers across the top of the figure correspond to those listed in Table 7.1. Note that planners do not expect the first defects to be discovered until about six months after the project begins. (It takes some time before the designers are far enough into high-level design to begin to find errors.)

out of three that measurements made as the project progresses will fall within the control limits.

Again, drawing projections and control limits for staff, defects, and code constructed would be a lot of work. But computers make it easy, as Figure 7.2 demonstrates.

Applying Statistical Control to Software Development

You are probably familiar with the application of statistical control to the manufacture of physical parts. Briefly, production engineers deem a part satisfactory if a critical dimension is either on target or within a small range of that target. Within that range, they consider the deviation from target to be normal. Measurements that fall within these control limits reflect the inherent instability of process machinery or measuring devices. Such parts are still good—they assemble with other parts satisfactorily. Occasionally a measurement falls outside the control limits. That means the machinery or measuring device has become deficient in some respect. Perhaps a tool has worn down. The out-of-limits measurement calls for investigation and corrective action.

We can apply the principle of statistical control to a knowledge process, such as software development, if we have a projection of what to expect and can lay control limits around it. We have just done that in Figure 7.2 for the defect rate. We could draw similar diagrams for staff and code construction. In fact, Figure 7.3 is such a diagram for staffing rate, except now we have added black circles to represent the actual staffing rate as the project progresses.

At first, the staff rate closely follows the expected plan, as shown on the left-hand side. The project is under control, that is, actual staffing is following planned staffing. On the right-hand diagram, however, actual staffing begins to exceed plan. The project is out of statistical control. If you are the project manager, you probably know why you are assigning more people than planned. For instance, changes to the requirements have increased the workload; or process productivity appears to be less than planned on, necessitating additional staff; or the work is more difficult than expected. Your issue becomes: can you get back on plan and finish within the overall estimates? Or should you replan the project?

If you are above the project-manager level, you want to find out what the project manager knows and what he or she is doing about it. The control chart alerts both of you. It lets you know, for example, if the customer is going to be affected; or resources

Statistical Control Methods

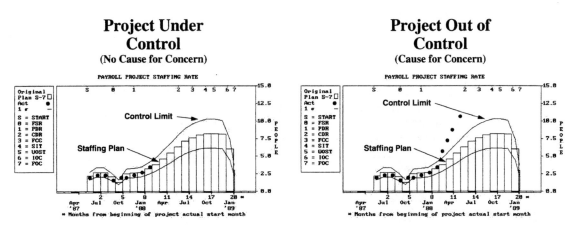

Figure 7.3 Software management can apply the basic principle of statistical control to the execution of a software project by monitoring actuals against projections of staff, defects, or code completed.

needed elsewhere are not going to be available as planned; or this project is going to eat up more staff, time, and money.

Monitoring the staffing rate of a project is a little different from monitoring the defect rate or code construction. Staffing rate is an input to the project that management determines. Defects and code are outputs that reflect whether the project is proceeding satisfactorily. Of course, if management does not staff according to plan, the outputs will no doubt be affected, too. In any event, when actuals begin to fall outside control limits, it is likely that something is going wrong. It is a signal to look into what that is.

In some instances, the project manager will find that he or she can correct the problem and get back on plan. He or she may need assistance from higher management. In other instances, it is unlikely that the project can be completed on the existing plan and must be replanned.

Replanning a Lagging Project

Replanning is based on the fact that further information about the project has become available. Usually, for new data to be meaningful, the project must have at least reached the critical-design-review milestone, or 25 percent of the main-build schedule. By this point, you can recalculate the process productivity the project is actually achieving, as compared to the process productivity that you calibrated or estimated, perhaps months ago.

Also, by this point, you know if requirements have expanded or the work to be accomplished appears to be greater than originally figured. You can increase the size estimate. Since the number of staff at peak will be an important influence on the new plan, you can revise that number, if necessary. A minor point, but one sometimes overlooked, is that if the project did not actually begin on the planned start date, you can realign that date.

With this new information, the computer is now able to lay out a new plan to completion, or to lay out several alternative plans for management judgment. If replanning takes place relatively early in development, such as at the 25-percent point, you can take advantage of the trade-off leverages described in Chapter 6. If the project is well along, however, on an unrealistic plan, there is little opportunity for trading off schedule time for less effort and fewer defects. This is because much of the effort has already been expended; many errors are already embedded in the design and code. People still have to complete the work; they still have to find and fix the defects; these efforts take personhours.

The Control Function

The ability to monitor project progress does not just fall out of the sky. It, too, has to be managed. Somebody or, in large organizations, several somebodies, have to do it.

The first step is to establish baselines for each project team by collecting data on past projects that the new control office can find.

Second, the control office works out procedures for collecting the basic metrics—those described in earlier chapters. With this data the various levels of management are in a position to carry out the practices we have suggested.

Of course, in an ideal world, everybody would cooperate in establishing the control office quickly and operating its metric procedures happily. In most worlds it helps if management itself is happy with the idea and participates in carrying it out.

In our experience, a control office takes about 1 percent of the resources being expended by a software organization. It can be fully established and functioning within six months.

The keys to good project tracking are defining measurable and countable entities and having a repeatable process for gathering and counting.

Edward F. Weller[4]

[1] R.B. Grady, "Successfully Applying Software Metrics," *Computer,* vol. 27, no. 9, Sept. 1994, pp. 18–25.

[2] L.H. Putnam and W. Myers, *Measures for Excellence: Reliable Software On Time, Within Budget,* Yourdon Press, Prentice-Hall, Englewood Cliffs, N.J., 1992.

[3] K. Whitaker, "Managing Software Maniacs," *American Programmer,* Dec. 1994, pp. 31–36.

[4] E.F. Weller, "Using Metrics to Manage Software Projects," *Computer,* vol. 27, no. 9, Sept. 1994, pp. 27–33.

Chapter 8

You May Not Realize—
How Poorly Organized the
Typical Software Company Is

"Studies have shown that for every six new large-scale software systems that are put into operation, two others are canceled," a staff writer for Scientific American *reported after a study of the field. "The average software development project overshoots its schedule by half; larger projects generally do worse. And some three-quarters of all large systems are 'operating failures,' that either do not function as intended or are not used at all."*

—*W. Wayt Gibbs*[1]

The article quoted above summarized a survey of 24 leading companies by the IBM Consulting Group. The companies developed large distributed systems. "The numbers were unsettling: 55 percent of the projects cost more than expected, 68 percent over-ran their schedules, and 88 percent had to be substantially redesigned."

The Software Engineering Institute at Carnegie Mellon University developed a scale of Capability Maturity Levels ranging from one to five, described briefly in Table 8.1. Of 284 software organizations assessed by 1994, 75 percent were at the lowest level, 16 percent at level 2, and 8 percent at level 3[2].

Our own data, Figure 8.1, reveals the number of business systems in each of more than 30 process-productivity index levels. Superimposed on the bar chart are the corresponding values of the Software Engineering Institute's five Capability Maturity Levels. Note that our data also shows a large proportion of systems in CMM level 1.

Note: The diagrams and tables in this chapter are based on data from more than 3,800 projects collected by QSM. This database, while large, is not necessarily representative of the entire software industry. A large percentage of the industry—perhaps as much as 75 percent—does not collect metrics and consequently cannot be represented in database collections. This large portion is believed to be less productive than the portion using metrics. Consequently, conclusions based on the reported metrics probably present a rosier picture of the state of the software industry than is actually the case.

Table 8.1   Process productivity and product quality improve as an organization moves from Level 1 of the Software Engineering Institute's Capability Maturity scale up to Level 5. In addition, the risk of not completing the system satisfactorily declines.

Level	Characteristic	Key process areas
5 Optimizing	Continuous focus on process improvement. Analysis of defect causes for feedback to process. Statistical evidence of effectiveness.	Defect prevention Technology innovation Process change management
4 Managed	*Quantitative* Process and quality measured, predictable, and within limits	Process measurement and analysis Quality management
3 Defined	*Qualitative* Process documented. Project progress and quality tracked.	Software product engr. Integrated management Training programs Intergroup coordination Peer reviews
2 Repeatable	*Intuitive* Process dependent on individuals repeating previous behavior	Requirements management Project planning/control Configuration management Subcontract management Quality assurance
1 Initial	*Ad hoc, chaotic* Process unstable Results unpredictable	

How much improvement is possible? As Figure 8.1 implies, a great deal. It is a long way from the low-productivity left end of the bar chart to the high-productivity right end of the chart. The question is: just how far in terms of process productivity? And just what is the productivity index that we use to denote process productivity?

Well, it is simply a set of index numbers presently running from 1 to 34 (the highest yet reported) that stand in for the raw process-productivity numbers that come out of the software equation tucked in a footnote in Chapter 2. The raw numbers run from 754 to 2,178,309. We thought users would be more comfortable with small index numbers, but the computer uses the raw numbers in its computations.

We should remember that this metric is not measuring just conventional productivity in the source-lines-of-code-per-personmonth sense; it is gauging the complex relationship between functionality (size), schedule, effort, reliability, and complexity.

QSM - SEI Mapping

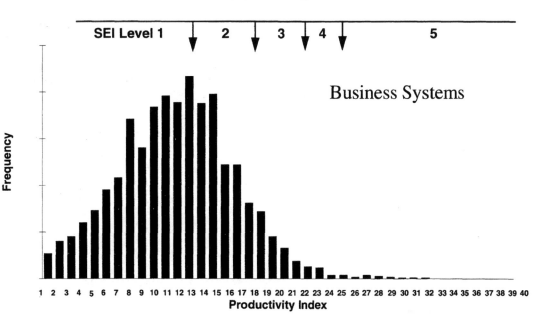

Figure 8.1 Distributing the process-productivity ratings of the business systems reported to us over 32 index levels demonstrates the broad sweep of organizational capability in this field. The SEI levels at the top of the chart show how they compare to our process-productivity index levels.

Productivity in this sense covers an enormous range: in this case a factor of 2889 between index number 1 and index number 34.

However, our database contains only a few organizations measured as high as 34. It would be more realistic to take an index of 25 (raw value: 242,786), where we have a large number of reports, as the high end. The process-productivity ratio (25 to 1, that is, 242,786 to 754) is 322, still a very large number.

It would be still more practical to look at the difference in process productivity between an organization one standard deviation below the mean and another organization one standard deviation above the mean. In other words, the difference between an organization at the 16th percentile and one at the 84th percentile in process productivity. This look drops out the cases at either end of the distribution and is more representative of the typical run of software organizations. In Table 8.2, we list the results for eight application categories.

Table 8.2 The right-hand column, headed Ratio, shows the factor of improvement for each application category between an organization at the 16th percentile and one at the 84th percentile. Note that as applications become more complex, from top to bottom, the mean productivity index declines.

Application category	Productivity index	Raw process productivity		Ratio
	Mean	16th percentile	84th percentile	
Business	16.2	11980	75025	6.26
Scientific	12.5	4675	32040	6.85
System software	11.3	3589	23245	6.48
Telecom	10.4	3391	15621	4.61
Process control	10.3	2584	20220	7.82
Command and control	9.9	2462	17711	7.19
Real time	6.8	1484	6605	4.45
Avionic	6.4	1258	6286	5.00
Average				6.08

The step from one index number to the next is substantial. The raw value of each index number is 1.27 times greater, on average, than the preceding value. Put another way, each index number represents a 27-percent increase in process productivity over the preceding number. Put in terms of schedule, effort, and reliability, one integer value of the productivity index is worth about 10 percent schedule reduction, 25 percent effort reduction, and 25 percent reliability improvement. Understanding that the step size is considerable becomes significant when we begin to talk of moving up the scale.

On the basis of these figures, it is safe to conclude that substantial improvement is possible for nearly all organizations—except perhaps a few at the very top of the present scale. Improvement is possible for most organizations, not because some great new "magic bullet" is coming down the pike, but because a substantial number of organizations are already doing better at the current level of technology. The implication is that everyone else can, too. However, new technology is in the pipeline. Even today's top-performing organizations can get better.

You May Not Realize—How Much Time It Takes to Improve

A few years ago, when excitement for "Total _____ Management" (fill in your own enthusiasm) was running high, several chief executive officers boldly went where no one had ventured before. They declared that various desirable software attributes would double or triple by Christmas or some other date certain not much further away than that. Since then, at least one of these bold venturers has been ventured out by action of his board of directors, though, to tell the truth, a weak software process was only one of his many problems.

Data reported to us since the mid-1970s indicates that the rate of software process improvement is slow in terms of executive hopes but fast compared to the growth rate of productivity in general. The best record for sustained improvement belongs to a company that we have been following since 1975, as detailed in the first line of Table 8.3. That record is 16 percent per year. Organizations building business systems average 10 percent per year. Engineering systems and real-time systems are still lower, as we would expect. All these percentages, however, are quite handsome compared with the two or three percent per year gain in manufacturing productivity.

In Figure 8.2, we extend this rate of improvement out through the decade of the 1990s for the business systems leader and the average developer and add, on the right-hand side, the Capability Maturity Levels. At the average rate of increase, organizations will take about a decade to advance from CMM Level 2 to Level 3. In doing so, however, they will climb through four productivity index numbers. Four goals to strive for during the decade offer more psychological encouragement than one goal.

Table 8.3   Process productivity increased during the 1980s as measured by our productivity index (PI). In percentage terms (last column) the gain has been impressive.

Application	Rate of improvement in process productivity		
	One PI every	PI/year	Percent/year
Business system best sustained record	1.5 years	0.67	16
Business systems average	2.5 years	0.40	10
Engineering systems*	3.0 years	0.33	8
Real-time systems	4.0 years	0.25	6

*Includes command and control systems, systems software, telecommunications systems, process control, and scientific software.

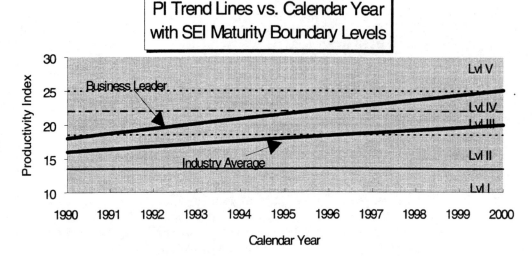

Figure 8.2   If past is prologue, the process-productivity trend lines will advance during the current decade at a goodly rate, but considerably short of unrealistic hopes.

You May Not Realize—How Good a Job the Software Industry Is Doing

When executives look at tables and figures like these, they are often disappointed. They see mountains of software to be developed and they don't see them turning into mole hills anytime soon. When Tom DeMarco, a well-known consultant to the industry, thinks of the last 30 years, he asks, "Where in hell did those expectations come from?" In contrast, he points out: "Out of thin air we made a $300 billion-a-year industry"[3].

Hard-headed businesspeople have been ponying up sums like that for many years and waiting in line to pony up still more—the software backlog. All the time they were complaining loudly. "I myself am a bit peeved by this," DeMarco admits. "I feel like we have accomplished wonders and been yelled at the whole time."

Of course, that is the nature of a competitive system. If one looks backward, one sees a terrific record. If one looks around, sharks appear on every side. If one looks forward, one sees an endless treadmill to ever higher performance—or a fall off the end of the treadmill to competitive oblivion.

IBM's software budget for 1966 was going to be forty million dollars. I asked Vin Learson . . . what he thought it would be and he said "Fifty million." This afternoon I met Watts Humphrey, who is in charge of programming production, in the hall here and said, "Is this figure about right? Can I use it?" He said, "It's going to be sixty million." You can see that if I keep asking questions we won't pay a dividend this year.

Thomas J. Watson Jr.[4]

[1] W.W. Gibbs, "Software's Chronic Crisis," *Scientific American,* Sept. 1994, pp. 86–95.

[2] J. Herbsleb et al., "Software Process Improvement: State of the Payoff," *American Programmer,* Sept. 1994, pp. 2–12.

[3] T. DeMarco, "Why Does Software Cost So Much?" *IEEE Software,* vol 10, no. 2, Mar. 1993, pp. 89–90.

[4] T.J. Watson, Jr. and P. Petre, *Father Son & Co. My Life at IBM and Beyond,* Bantam Books, New York, 1990.

Chapter 9

The Key Process Metric: Process Productivity

We need a concept of productivity that considers together all the efforts that go into output and expresses them in relation to their result. . . . First, there is knowledge— man's most productive resource if properly applied. . . . Then there is time—man's most perishable resource.

Peter Drucker[1]

The process-productivity metric is the key to the control of the process-improvement process itself. As we showed in previous chapters, about three-quarters of the software organizations assessed so far are in the initial Level 1 of the Software Engineering Institute's Capability Maturity scale. On our process-productivity-index scale, half are below average—no great surprise statistically speaking! But half are above average and some are very, very good. Again, no great surprise to the statistically minded. We bring the point up only to emphasize that organizations with excellent software development processes do exist. That high level is possible at the current state of software technology.

The question for this chapter is how to control the process of getting there. The question sounds simple, but the experience of many organizations demonstrates that managing process improvement is not easy. For example, the Software Engineering Institute assessed the Standard Systems Center of the Air Force Communications Command at Maxwell Air Force Base, Alabama, at Capability Maturity Level 1 in 1987.

In response, the Center initiated an improvement program. Process Action Teams made many excellent analyses and pointed out ways to improve. Five years later, despite these efforts, the Center as a whole remained at Level 1. When we analyzed the Center's situation in 1993, we noted many reasons for this lack of progress. One major concern was balancing the investment cost of instilling methodology and processes against the return on investment that should result.

Indeed, Herb Krasner reported that "many formal software process-improvement programs which attempted to start in the late 80's faltered soon after a formal assessment was performed (two thirds reportedly died), are now in decline, or perhaps will soon fail"[2]. So the issue is not just an unfocused desire to improve the software process, but how to do it successfully.

What It's Like When You Get There

Most of you have a first-hand feeling for what it is like to work in or manage a chaotic, unpredictable Level 1 organization, because that is where most of you are currently serving your time. After a few years, you tend to think, "This is what life in the software trenches is." Instead, let us hold out a vision of what it's like in the higher-level organizations.

You can predict schedule, effort, and reliability and generally accomplish your plans. Your numbers are better than your competitors, so you get work. With work in-house and proceeding according to plan, you have the resources to acquire, train, motivate, and keep good people. Their talents flourish. They keep up with advances in technology. Your processes continue to improve. A life like this in software isn't such a bad thing after all.

Your Starting Level

Formally establishing your Capability Maturity level is a large order. A trained team has to come to your site and spend several days assessing it. Sometimes you can shortcut this approach by finding an individual in your organization who has read some of the Software Engineering Institute's material and is able to guess what level you are on—usually Level 1. But Level 1 embraces over half of all software organizations. For control purposes you need a more precise measure.

That could be process productivity, as measured by our productivity index. All you need to find your index number is the management numbers on a few recently completed projects: size, schedule time, and effort. With this data a computer program calculates the productivity index. When we did this at the Standard Systems Center, for example, we found the levels summarized in Table 9.1. With the exception of the first project in the table, the other six are in the average range for business systems. In fact, three are above the average productivity index of 16.

When assessed as an overall organization, the Center appeared to be mired in Capability Maturity Level 1. When we looked at individual projects, we found pockets of superior performance, several as high as Level 3. This performance appears to have evolved as the result of local initiative.

The exceptionally low project, at a productivity index of 4.6, is the result of special circumstances, rather than an especially deficient software process. For instance,

Table 9.1   Seven business systems at the Standard Systems Center had productivity indexes and corresponding estimated Capability Maturity Levels extending over a wide range.

Project name	Productivity index	Capability maturity level
Enhancement to supply system	4.6	1
Inventory reporting subsystem	19.1	3
Budget history retrieval system	15.3	2
Extension to budget system	13.4	1
Budget transition system	13.8	2
Police blotter system	17.3	2
Real property management	19.0	3

16 major commands had to agree on the specifications and changes had to be approved by a high-level board, which met only every six months. It was a small project, only 10,500 lines, mostly in Cobol, but difficulties in fitting this piece into a very old existing system increased effort. The stretched-out time and increased effort resulted in the low productivity index.

When you have the productivity index of a sample of recent projects, you can compare them against the mean productivity indexes of different application categories, as previously listed in Table 8.2. A database covering thousands of systems in different application areas would enable your technical people to make more detailed comparisons. You can see how urgently, in terms of competition, you need to improve your software process.

Your Process Improvement Program

You probably suspect already that there are several things you could do right away. Your people know some other things to do, like getting rid of bottlenecks. Move up to better third-generation languages, fourth-generation languages, and application generators. Move from batch development on centralized mainframes to interactive development on individual workstations. Get the new software tools you know you should have obtained long ago. Record at least the basic management numbers (size, development time, effort, defect rate) in a retrievable manner.

In short, get up to date. Don't try to get out in front at this point. We have seen organizations move up one productivity index number, sometimes two or three, just by removing bottlenecks that were delaying their people.

Getting beyond the obvious next steps takes more planning. Most organizations set up a small central group to ride herd on process improvement. Sometimes it is called the software engineering process group, and sometimes the process assurance group, or a process action team. To give you an idea of the scope of this effort, the Software Engineering Institute recommends devoting three to five percent of total software development costs to process improvement. Only a small part of that figure goes to support the central group; most goes to support training and other efforts throughout the entire software organization.

That brings up the matter of funding the improvement program. Part of the funding, for training, for example, is expense-type money. Another part, for equipment or expensive software tools, may be capitalized. These funds may require approval at a high organizational level. Getting approval usually requires evidence that the capital invested will bring at least a minimum return on investment. You can estimate the investment side of that proposition with some precision, but arriving at an estimate of the savings that will result from the investment is more difficult. It is especially so in the case of software development. More on how to do this a little later.

Control of Process Improvement

At this point, you know at what level of process productivity your recent projects have been running. You have a process improvement program getting under way. If you wish, you can set a goal for the next few years. Above all, the goal should be realistic. If you set some extreme goal, you lose credibility with your people.

For example, for a time a few years back there was talk of applying Motorola's Six Sigma goal—3.4 defects per million opportunities to err—to software development. That goal, depending on how one defines it, is several orders of magnitude beyond current software achievement levels. Yet some executives directed their people to get there in two years. That was unrealistic. In these circumstances, the troops tend to linger in the trenches, rather than go over the top.

More realistic goals are in the vicinity of the average improvements achieved in the last 10 years, such as one productivity-index point every 2.5 years for business systems, as listed in Table 8.3 or visualized for the 1990s in Figure 8.2. You can draw a statistical control chart of the improvement rate you decide on, bordered by control limits.

Then, as projects are completed, you can plot them on the chart. Not all projects will achieve the expected goal line. As we saw in the case of the Standard Systems Center, some will do better and some will do worse. If they are within the control limits, the deviation may be normal. If a project falls below the lower limit, it bears looking into. Something went wrong, as in the case of the low ranking project at the Standard

Systems Center. Or perhaps the project team needs special help in improving its process. You know where your problems are.

Figuring Return on Investment

You can use the improvement in process productivity over time to estimate the savings that your process improvement is returning. The Real Property Management system, previously listed in Table 9.1, provides a case in point. This system comprised 105,000 lines of new Cobol code. It became operational in October 1990. At that time the actual management numbers, listed in Table 9.2, represented a productivity index of 19.0, equivalent to a Capability Maturity Level of 3. We have assumed, perhaps arbitrarily, that this system, if done when the Standard Systems Center was first assessed in 1987, would have carried a productivity index of 13.4, in Level 1.

The improvement in cost over this four-year period was ($788,000 – $142,000) or $646,000. This is the savings. If we had a figure for the investment over this period applicable to this project, we could calculate the return on investment. In this case, we do not have an investment figure.

However, Krasner has searched for companies with successful process improvement programs and reports: "ROI figures between 5 to 1 and 9 to 1 . . . . The payoff is delayed in time, sometimes by as much as several years, due to the complexities of institutionalization and culture change. This delay can stress the attention spans of short term, delivery oriented, crisis driven, middle managers whose support is necessary for software process improvement to flourish"[2].

Table 9.2 The management numbers at which the Real Property Management system was accomplished (column 2) are much better than the numbers at which it might have been done four years earlier (column 1). The third column shows the ratio of improvement resulting from the gain in process productivity.

Management numbers	Before Level 1	Actual Level 3	Benefit ratio
Time, months	29	17	1.7
Effort, personmonths	206	37	5.6
Cost, $	788,000	142,000	5.6
Peak staff	10	3	3.2
Mean time to defect, days	3	10	3.2

In addition to return on investment, the Standard System Center has greatly improved the time it takes to reach operational status and system reliability—both improvements not easily reduced to dollar savings.

Challenging but Doable

Our experience in the field tells us that many software people and managers find it hard to believe that they can achieve this degree of process improvement. "The laggards do not measure," Capers Jones noted, "and so they do not have a clue as to how good or bad they are." We might add further—they don't have a clue as to how good they could get[3].

"In truth, in spite of the stories of how rough it is out there, a lot of managers have not really been very hard pressed," observed Tom Gilb, with 20 years of worldwide consulting experience to draw lessons from[4].

Perhaps the knowledge that process improvement is going on all around them will press them harder in the future. It is a challenging activity, but it is doable. You can convince yourself by setting a reasonable rate of improvement, perhaps one productivity-index point every two or three years, then checking to see if you are accomplishing it.

Performance measurement is an essential ingredient of any study that purports to help managers learn how to improve the functioning of their organizations.

Thomas J. Allen[5]

[1] P.F. Drucker, *Management: Tasks, Responsibilities, Practices,* Harper & Row, New York, 1973.

[2] H. Krasner, "The Payoff for Software Process Improvement: What It Is and How to Get It," *Software Process Newsletter,* IEEE Computer Society, Sept. 1994, pp. 3–8.

[3] C. Jones, "What Differentiates Leaders from Laggards," *Application Development Trends,* Jan. 1995, pp. 27–31.

[4] T. Gilb, "Fighting Ambiguity One Document At A Time," *IEEE Software,* vol. 11, no. 1, Jan. 1994, pp. 104–105.

[5] T.J. Allen, *Managing the Flow of Technology: Technology Transfer and the Dissemination of Technological Information Within the R&D Organization,* The MIT Press, Cambridge, Mass., 1977.

Chapter 10

Managing Development Contracts with the Process-Productivity Metric

After performing software assessments for 20 or so companies, an ominous pattern begins to emerge. In company after company . . . formal methods and tools used by management as the basis for sizing, planning, estimating, and tracking major software projects are often close to nonexistent.

Capers Jones[1]

The software development contractor to whom you are about to entrust the family fortune may be one of those seat-of-the-pants operators. How do you know if a supplier fully understands your requirements? Has the supplier correctly converted the requirements to the amount of work to be done, that is, to the size of the eventual system? Has the supplier established a schedule and staff effort sufficient to build a system of that size? Does the supplier have inspection and test practices that assure a quality product? Or is he or she just parroting back what you want to hear?

One way to establish a supplier's bona fides is past performance—whether he or she has performed well for you, or someone you know, in the past. A good record implies that a good performance is repeatable. Another way is to send a few good people out to the supplier's premises to ask a set of questions. Nosing around is easy, but making an accurate judgment of a supplier's capability in this way is not. A better way is to apply the methods we have been outlining for your own use to suppliers as well.

Evaluate Potential Suppliers

Before you look for suppliers, you can establish reasonable performance goals for the project. At this stage, of course, requirements may not be complete. You may be able to estimate only very wide bounds for the eventual size of the system. You don't know who is going to do the work, so you don't know what their process productivity is.

However, you can establish an expected size for the system. You can use the average process productivity for the application type. You can assume a midrange manpower buildup rate. With this data, you can estimate the range within which the development time and effort will fall. You now have an idea of what qualifications you need in a supplier if he or she is to meet this schedule and budget.

If the supplier is to perform as you hope, the process productivity of his or her organization must be in the vicinity of the productivity index number you used in your preliminary analysis. There is only one way to find out. You must be prepared to ask possible suppliers what their management numbers—size, effort, development time—were on three or four recently completed systems. With this information, you can calculate the supplier's process productivity.

Unfortunately, not every company keeps track of even these basic metrics. Unfortunately for you, you may sometimes have to deal with such companies—because there are a lot of them out there. Even if they record some numbers, they may not have defined them carefully or disciplined their organizations to carry out regular collection. Even if they recorded something during the project, the information may be for all practical purposes inaccessible—buried in several file boxes of old project records.

If a supplier's metrics are not very good, it is still possible to estimate its process productivity with a set of questions. The margin of error of such an estimate is larger than one obtained by calibration of past metrics, but it is better than flying blind.

With information of this sort, you are able to disqualify suppliers who appear quite unsuited to develop the proposed system. Note that you are not barring any supplier arbitrarily, you are acting on the basis of their own past performance numbers—quite objective data.

The rest are given the opportunity to bid. You ask them to include in their proposals their estimate of the size of the proposed system and the schedule, as well as cost and staff effort.

With the arrival of proposals, you have this productivity information with which to judge the contestants. Are their estimates of size in line with your own? If not, do they have a convincing analysis to support their own estimate? Given their estimate of size and their historic process productivity, is their projection of schedule and effort realistic? From their size, schedule, and effort estimates, you can calculate the process productivity they would have to achieve to carry out their proposal. Is this number in line with their historic number?

When you have this kind of information to work with, the low bid may not be attractive, just unrealistic. The supplier with a realistic schedule and cost is more likely to produce a satisfactory product on time and within budget.

Bidding an Engineering System

We have had many opportunities over the years to apply these ideas to actual bidding situations. Here is one, involving an engineering system, covering work from requirements to acceptance test. The system included five functional subsystems. The sponsor's initial size estimate, with requirements still in flux, was a range: 270,000 to 370,000 source lines of code. He had about $6.5 million available. He wanted the system in 16 months.

Our first step was to see what kind of process productivity an organization would have to have to carry out the sponsor's desired numbers. The solution is listed in column 1 of Table 10.1.

The productivity index needed to accomplish the project on the sponsor's hopes was 21.2. The average productivity index of organizations building engineering systems is 11; the standard deviation is 4. The chance of finding a supplier with a level of capability greater than 21 is very small. Similarly, a manpower buildup index of 5.4 is very fast. To build up at this rate, an organization would have to break down the work very rapidly and have people standing by to take it on at once—an assumption we cannot count on.

In column 2 of Table 10.1, we assume a productivity index a little above the mean and a manpower buildup index in the middle range. This much less capable organization would take more than twice as long at about three times the effort and cost. With a much reduced productivity index, this organization is much less skilled at avoiding or correcting defects. The mean time to defect at delivery is about one-sixth that of the highly effective organization. These are not happy answers, but they are realistic. Somewhere around average is where most software development organizations actually are.

Table 10.1 Column 1 lists the numbers for the scenario originally envisioned by the engineering system's sponsor. Column 2 shows the realistic numbers that a real-life supplier might be able to accomplish.

Management number	1 Original	2 Realistic
Size SLOC	351,690	351,690
Development time, months	16	34
Effort, personmonths	711	2129
Cost, $	6,520,000	19,516,000
Peak staff	62	85
Mean time to defect, days	1.84	.31
Productivity index	21.2	12.2
Manpower buildup index	5.4	2.3

Monitoring Progress

In the course of gathering the management numbers and making these analyses, you will very likely have the opportunity to discuss what they mean with some of the competing suppliers. In the process, they may learn something about making better supported bids.

In the case of the winning bidder, having a friendly relationship will help in the next stage. During the execution of the project, you will be expecting monthly progress updates. Quarterly updates may be sufficient for a very large project extending over several years. With these reports, you monitor and control the supplier's progress along the same lines as we outlined in Chapter 7 for internal control.

For example, in 1985, we were retained as consultants by a government agency to prepare a "should cost" shadow bid. The agency wanted this bid as a check on the bids it was receiving from suppliers. Unfortunately, it had none of the management numbers on its bidders. Worse, its rules did not permit it to get the numbers. Its contract administrators were not allowed to place any demands on bidders that cost money to comply. We had no choice but to compute the shadow bid on the basis of average process productivity for the application—a very large engineering system.

Even so, it was plainly apparent that the three-year schedule imposed by the agency and accepted by the top bidders was grossly unrealistic. Over the years since then, we have performed several tracking and control updates. In each case the schedule had already slipped. Effort and cost were already higher than planned. Our projections generally showed that schedule would have to be extended 9 to 12 months. The agency and the supplier usually agreed on a 2 or 3 month extension. By the time they had agreed on this minuscule correction, the project was already beyond the new date.

As we are putting the case here, it makes the people who were involved sound stupid. Of course, they weren't. They were just people under pressure. Higher levels of management, which in this case were political people—appointees and legislative committees—wouldn't pay much attention to a few months slippage but they would to a year or more. That would be long enough to be embarrassing; long enough to get in the papers.

At the time of this writing, it is 10 years later. We haven't been consulted for many years, but we still read about the project in the papers. It still hasn't finished. We hasten to add that this project involved many problems beyond planning and scheduling. Technical problems turned up that were not originally anticipated. The size and functionality has greatly increased over the years. Nevertheless, grossly inaccurate estimates, both originally and in periodic updates, contributed to the debacle.

Supplier Improvement Program

As a supplier becomes accustomed to a customer assessing bids and monitoring progress, the idea of improving the software development process itself comes into focus. A cooperative relationship for this purpose is a relatively new idea in the United States, but it is not unknown. Companies are beginning to substitute long-term working-together patterns for the competitive bid one-shot pattern.

To cite one example, "Since 1982, Bell Canada Corporate Quality Assurance has been assessing the software product development process of prospective suppliers as a means to minimize the risks involved and ensure both the performance and timely delivery of purchased software systems," reported Francois Coallier. "The presence of an efficient-capability continuous-improvement program in a supplier is, for Bell Canada, a reassuring sign of organizational maturity. Being invited to participate in such a program is a sign, from a supplier quality-management perspective, of high maturity in the customer-supplier partnership"[2].

The process-productivity view of software development reveals that organizations can make orders-of-magnitude gains in efficiency, albeit getting such gains takes a few years. At best, the competitive-bid approach can gain only small percentages between one average bidder and another. If you have to take the lowest bidder, regardless of other considerations, you are likely to get a low-quality product very late at an overrun cost. In quite a few cases, you spend the money, wait the time, and get no product.

To really trust people to perform, you must be aware of their progress.

Watts S. Humphrey[3]

[1] C. Jones, "Software Management: The Weakest Link in the Software Engineering Chain," *Computer,* vol. 27, no. 5, May 1994, pp. 10–11.

[2] F. Coallier, "Trillium: A Model for the Assessment of Telecom Product Development & Support Capability," *Software Process Newsletter,* Winter 1995, pp. 3–8.

[3] W.S. Humphrey, *Managing the Software Process,* Addison-Wesley Publishing Co., Reading, Mass., 1989.

Chapter 11

Process Improvement: Organizational and Personal

*In the old days, if you were a bricklayer who got promoted to CEO of brickmaking,
you pretty much knew what a brick was and if somebody came to you with an idea,
you'd know whether it was a good idea or a bad idea.*

Scott Adams, creator of the comic strip, Dilbert[1]

Our experience with hundreds of software organizations tells us that many software people and managers find it hard to believe that the software process is improvable to the degree that leading companies have actually accomplished. Of course, there are good reasons for this belief. As a point of fact, most companies have not improved very much. People look around them and what they see confirms their pessimism.

The feeling that software development is an art and that it depends on getting and keeping talented artists is still widespread. "In our little off-the-beaten-track company, how can we hope to get the best software artists?" software managers tell themselves. "We don't have the funding. We can't afford to pay the salaries that top-notch people get."

A long series of hyped-up tools and methods have led many to feel that a technological fix for the problems of software development was in the offing. Not so, quoth the seer, Fred Brooks. "As we look to the horizon of a decade hence," he wrote in 1987, "we see no silver bullet. There is no single development, in either technology or in management technique, that by itself promises even one order-of-magnitude improvement in productivity, in reliability, in simplicity"[2].

As we near the end of Brooks's decade-horizon, his foresight was sound. No single development was the magic bullet. But, somehow, leading developers are orders of magnitude better than the laggards. We contend that they have accomplished this feat, not by magic, but by plugging away at one step after another. The steps are

67

available to any plugger. Pluggers are stepping in two directions: organization-wide and personal.

Improve the Organization

People have been improving the software process ever since the 1950s, when the more understandable assembly language replaced nearly incomprehensible (to human beings) machine language. The idea of managing the improvement process took a great leap forward in 1989, when Watts S. Humphrey of the Software Engineering Institute at Carnegie Mellon University published *Managing the Software Process*[3].

This was the book that introduced the five Capability Maturity Levels that we summarized in Table 8.1. Humphrey viewed the five levels as a path that would guide organizations striving to improve their software process. The idea caught on. The five levels were also a sort of grading system. Managers could try for a better grade. Moving up one grade in five was something within reach.

Gerald M. Weinberg, possibly in a fit of irony, added a new initial level to the five-level model and renamed the other levels[4]:

Oblivious:	"We don't even know that we're performing a process."
Variable:	"We do whatever we feel like at the moment."
Routine:	"We follow our routines (except when we panic)."
Steering:	"We choose among our routines by the results they produce."
Anticipating:	"We establish routines based on our past experience with them."
Congruent:	"Everyone is involved in improving everything all the time."

Many other organizations have also issued models or standards, as listed in Table 11.1. However, we don't expect you, as a busy executive or manager, to read this much material. We cite them merely as an indication that people have devoted a lot of thought to the issue of improving the software process. Our immediate question is what can a busy executive do about it.

This is probably not the first time you have had to initiate action to improve efficiency. What did you do the other times? Likely something similar to the following.

Plan.   In technical situations, figuring out what to do is often too complicated for one person to do by himself or herself. You have to blend the contributions of executives, first-line managers, and technology specialists (who are familiar with the kind of material represented by the documents in Table 11.1). Some people urge that representatives of working developers or programmers be involved, especially on issues of

Table 11.1 An organization planning a process-improvement program may consider a number of models and standards:

Capability Maturity Model for Software, Version 1.1 (latest version of the Humphrey model), Software Engineering Institute, Carnegie Mellon University, Pittsburgh, PA;

ISO 9000-3, Guidelines for the Application of ISO 9001 to the Development, Supply, and Maintenance of Software, International Organization for Standardization, Geneva, Switzerland;

TickIT: A Guide to Software Quality Management System Construction and Certification Using EN29001, United Kingdom Department of Trade and Industry, London;

Malcolm Baldrige National Quality Awards Criteria, Department of Commerce, Washington, DC;

Bellcore FA-NWT-000179 Standard and FA-NWT-001315 Document;

IEEE Software Engineering Standards Collection;

Sematech SOI model;

Motorola QSR/SEI Challenge;

AT&T Process Quality Model;

QIP (Quality Improvement Paradigm) model, Software Engineering Laboratory, University of Maryland;

Trillium Assessment Model, Bell Canada.

particular importance to them. Similarly, some issues affect customers and it may be helpful to have their point of view represented.

We are not particularly recommending the models listed in the table in their entirety, though there is much helpful guidance in them. Various experts have expressed dissatisfaction with them and they may not be well matched to your particular set of problems. It is up to you and your task force to work out a plan that effectively addresses your situation.

Act. With a plan in hand, much of your action can take place through your regular hierarchical organization. But the line of command is often preoccupied with day-to-day business. To compensate, many organizations have felt the need to establish an action group, such as a Software Engineering Process Group, to put special and continuing emphasis on process improvement. Moreover, when a champion of some particular approach arises almost spontaneously, help him or her. Don't frown just because he or she is outside the normal chain of command. Try to figure out how to take advantage of such enthusiasm.

Change.   Human beings resist change. Organizations resist change. Bureaucratic organizations—those with a hierarchy of executives, managers, and worker bees—resist change more effectively than more free-wheeling organizations. In a bureaucratic organization, all the levels have to be convinced of the value of a change and have to act in concert to pull it off. In the empowered organization, of which we have heard much in recent years, individuals, small groups, quality circles, and the like are supposed to have more power to do something new on their own initiative.

Support.   Whatever kind of organization you have, executive support helps the change process. Beyond verbal flag waving, you can manifest this support in three ways. Where improvement takes some funding, either for investment in capital equipment or for training, step forward. (That doesn't mean you finance everything willy-nilly. One of the realities your plan was supposed to take into account was matching the pace of improvement to the available funding. Don't overlook the fact that the savings resulting from increased productivity give you more money to play with.) Second, where your people report the results in figures, look at them and show interest. Third, where improvement takes time (it always does), maintain continuity of support.

Control.   One of the features of your plan will certainly be measurement. It provides the basis for projecting results numerically and monitoring whether they are indeed taking place. The fact that you regularly monitor these results is a key way of demonstrating continuing interest. Moreover, if the results are favorable, they assure you that process improvement is on the right track. You will feel more comfortable pursuing the plan.

Personal Software Process

"The introduction of improved software methods is often slow because software engineers must be personally convinced of the effectiveness of new methods before they will consistently use them," Humphrey told the Conference on the Software Process in 1994. "Few software engineers are aware of or consistently practice the best available methods. The initial data (from his Personal Software Process research) show that very few engineers use such proven practices as disciplined design methods, design or code reviews, or defined testing procedures"[5].

The Personal Software Process, as explained in Humphrey's book, consists of seven steps, such as "begin to measure own work," "measure size," and "plan schedule"[6]. The text tells in some detail how to do these things, but the real payoff comes in the 10 problems. Each problem not only requires the software engineer to program a problem illustrating one of the steps, but also to measure pertinent metrics pertaining to his or her programming effort. With data on his or her own work rate derived from the first few problems, the engineer can project, for example, the schedule for a later problem. Thus, the engineer both learns better methods and is convinced of increased efficiency by measurement of his or her own work.

Carrying out the Personal Software Process, however, is not easy. On the average, working each problem takes four hours. In addition, there is study time and class time. Humphrey recommends that companies allow an engineer a full day a week to keep up. He says flatly: "Attempts by engineers to learn these PSP methods by reading this book and then trying to apply the techniques on their projects have not worked." He feels strongly that the discipline of a course, instructor, and formal assignments is necessary.

Data from the first few courses (50 participants) indicate that defects found in test were reduced by a factor of 10. The course emphasizes finding defects early by means of reviews and inspections. Productivity improved by 35 percent. Funds expended on the course are soon recovered by gains of this magnitude.

At the same time, the Personal Software Process, as valuable as it is, "should not be viewed as a replacement for an organization process improvement effort," Humphrey believes. "The two, in fact, are quite complementary. However, organizations near the CMM process maturity level 2—the repeatable level—or above are likely to be most successful in introducing the Personal Software Process"[6].

In our hype-ridden society (just this morning we have had two calls from telephone marketeers, one promising to increase our wealth and the other to enhance our home security) we are not easily persuaded. The best way executives and managers can convince themselves that they can improve the software process is to measure the process productivity of successive projects and see for themselves.

While you can read all that I or anyone else says on the subject, the only way to convince yourself is to measure your own [work] and see for yourself.

Watts Humphrey[6]

[1] D. Brittan, "Interview: Scott Adams, 'Gadfly of the High-Tech Workplace,'" *Technology Rev.,* Jan. 1995, pp. 22–29.

[2] F.P. Brooks, Jr., "No Silver Bullet: Essence and Accidents of Software Engineering," *Computer,* vol. 20, no. 4, April 1987, pp. 10–19.

[3] W.S. Humphrey, *Managing the Software Process,* Addison-Wesley Publishing Co., Reading, Mass., 1989.

[4] G.M. Weinberg, *Quality Software Management: Vol. 1, Systems Thinking,* Dorset House Publishing, New York, 1992.

[5] W.S. Humphrey, "The Personal Process in Software Engineering," *Proc. Third Int'l Conf. on the Software Process,* IEEE Computer Society Press, Los Alamitos, Calif., 1994, pp. 69–77.

[6] W.S. Humphrey, *A Discipline for Software Engineering,* Addison-Wesley Publishing Co., Reading, Mass., 1995.

Chapter 12

Putting It All Together

The fundamental issues of software management are no different from any other domain: understand the problem, manage people, manage quality, manage cost, manage schedule, anticipate problems, and control damage.

Carl K. Chang[1]

Except for the planet itself, there is nothing on Earth older than living systems. "Many natural systems, especially living ones, show a quality usually called adaptation," Arthur D. Hall, a systems engineer at Bell Telephone Laboratories, reminded us a generation ago. "That is, they possess the ability to react to their environments in a way that is favorable, in some sense, to the continued operation of the systems"[2]. That is really something old.

Science and engineering have long appreciated a concept called feedback. Briefly, this technique measures some attribute of the output of a process and returns it to the input of the process to affect what goes on in the process and ultimately to produce a better output. This, too, is something old.

Early in this century, Walter Shewhart, also at Bell Telephone Laboratories, originated the cycle: Plan, Do, Check, and Act. That is, in view of the deficiencies uncovered in the Check stage, Act to revise the Plan to correct them—and thus continue the improvement cycle indefinitely. A little later, W. Edwards Deming (born 1900) and J.M. Juran (born 1904) extended the Shewhart Cycle to quality improvement. On a grander scale, our economic system itself feeds back information from the marketplace to the enterprise to improve both product and process. Again, these "processes to improve processes" are something old.

Something New

The application of methods such as these to the improvement of the several phases of software development is fairly new. Of course, people have been thinking of better methods of programming computers since the first one was switched on. For feedback control purposes, however, they have been handicapped by the lack of a good metric characterizing the output of the software development process.

A count of source lines of code per personmonth, while superficially analogous to shoes per shoemaker-month, has several major weaknesses. An obvious one is that it does not measure the quality of the code. If organizations put too much emphasis on the count, programmers may, more or less subconsciously, increase the count at the expense of quality. Less obvious is the fact that source lines of code per personmonth does not reflect the effects of the relationship between schedule, effort, and project size. Process productivity, obtained by calibration from these three management numbers, embodies all the influences—management capability, tool investment, method usage, reusability, people motivation, product complexity, and so forth—that enable an organization to develop a software product on a shorter schedule, with less effort and greater reliability.

Project Estimation

Initially, a customer expresses its needs for a software product in the form of some kind of requirements, probably not fully thought through. Or, in the case of a market of many potential customers, the software organization's own marketing structure attempts to work out some requirements. Refer to Figure 12.1. Working with the customer or representatives of a marketplace, the software organization reduces the requirements to a more precisely stated specification. It carries out at least the first stages of functional design to the point where it has some idea of the product for which it is to estimate size, schedule, budget, and reliability.

From a database of management numbers of past projects, the estimators calibrate the process productivity that will apply to the proposed work, as discussed in Chapter 2. They estimate the size of the proposed product, per Chapter 3.

With these two numbers in hand, and with indications of the constraints of people, budget, schedule, and reliability that apply to the work, they can make preliminary estimates of schedule, effort, and cost, as Chapter 4 explains. They can forecast the defect rate to be expected during the project and the number of defects likely to be in the product at the time of delivery, according to Chapter 5.

In Chapter 6, we saw that schedule and effort could be traded off, that is, a little more development time leads to less effort, less cost, a smaller staff, and fewer defects. At this point we have reached a realistic estimate of what can actually be accomplished. Then, depending on management's judgment of the customer or the market, the responsible manager may modify the estimate into the final bid. The responsible man-

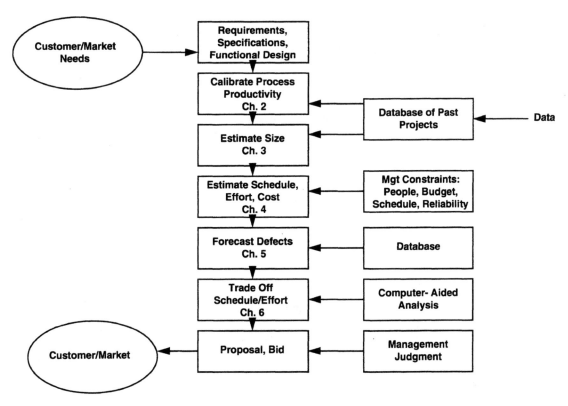

Figure 12.1   Process productivity plays a key role in the estimation process.

ager knows what has to be done, but he or she also knows, within some margin of risk, the reality the project is up against.

Monitor and Control

Let's say that the project gets the go-ahead. From the estimated management numbers, project leaders can project tables or curves of the rates of money expenditure, staff or effort assignment, defect occurrence, and code production, as suggested in Figure 12.2. These rates serve as the expected mean line and control limits on statistical control charts, as outlined in Chapter 7. So long as the actual rates are within the control limits, management can be confident that the project is proceeding as expected. An actual number near or outside the control limits warns that the project is deviating from plan.

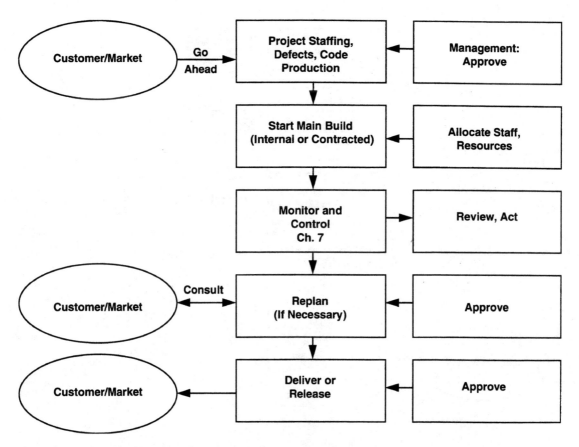

Figure 12.2 The building of a software product follows a process that can be subjected to monitoring and statistical control.

Appropriate action may return the work to plan. In some cases management may find it necessary, often in consultation with the customer or representatives of the market, to replan the project.

Compilation of Management Numbers

At the end of the project, in addition to a victory party, two further tasks are important. Unfortunately, they are often neglected, possibly because the following project is already behind schedule!

One task is the collection of the management numbers actually accomplished on the project. If an organization has defined its metrics, disciplined its collection process, and dinned the importance of metrics into every participant's skull, the return of the actual numbers to the database of past projects, shown in Figure 12.1, is relatively simple. In the database, they are easily accessible for use on future projects. If an organization has been a bit lax about its metric discipline, project management may have to exercise some judgment about the numbers to file in the database. Some numbers are better than no numbers.

The second task is postmortem analysis. What the project team has learned should be recorded, not so much for posterity as for feedback.

Process Improvement

An organization can accomplish its estimates only if it has a software development process that it can repeat. An organization can stay in business into the 21st century only if it has a process that it can successively improve. We can only suggest the complexity of the improvement process in Figure 12.3.

Basically, the various inspection, review, and test activities can highlight deficiencies in the development process. These deficiencies can be traced to causes, an activity called causal analysis. These causes can then be corrected, perhaps by direct referral back to the software process, if the cause is specific. Or, if the cause is more general, by referral to the task force for process improvement. The task force, under management guidance, can then undertake the investment or training needed to remove the cause.

On the right side of the figure, postmortem analysis can also reveal deficiencies that can be treated in the same way. In addition to the more formal mechanisms of causal analysis and postmortem analysis, anyone may call attention to a deficiency encountered in the course of work. Moreover, the task force on its own initiative will devise a series of plans to improve the software process.

Driving the whole process-improvement process is process productivity. The process schematized in Figure 12.3 is driven by management at the left. But what drives management? Visible signs of getting somewhere. That visible sign is measured process productivity increasing from one project to the next, as process improvement activities are carried out.

Results through People

We've put a great deal of emphasis on process. Our diagrams in this chapter make up, in effect, an interlocking series of processes, measured and controlled by process productivity. It is a good approach and we highly recommend it.

Nevertheless, there is another side to process. As expressed by Graham Sharman, a senior partner in McKinsey & Co., in the Wall Street Journal, "It is remarkable how

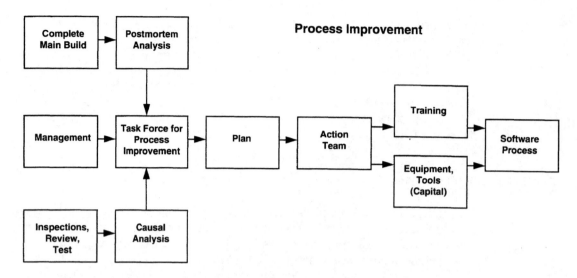

Figure 12.3 Ways to improve the software arise out of the work itself as a result of inspection and test and out of postmortem analysis of a project. Still more improvements can be initiated by management through a task force and action teams.

often the focus with process diverts attention from results and creates excess staff and bureaucracy"[3].

Ah, those forbidding words, "excess staff and bureaucracy." Put that way, we shudder. But behind those revulsion-inspiring words are what? Just people, and software development is a people business. You can get more powerful computers; you can install client-server networks; you can go object-oriented. But software development is at base an activity in which people have to think, as IBM epitomized long ago in its ubiquitous sign: Think.

We all remember Parkinson's Law: work expands to fill the time allocated for it. Tom DeMarco and Timothy Lister show that the law "almost certainly" doesn't apply to software people. They do believe, however, that a slight variation of the law is true in many organizations: "Organizational busy work tends to expand to fill the working day"[4].

Like that age-old question, "who will watch the guardians?" we can ask, who will watch the process improvers? Management, that's who. And how will they do it? By watching the numbers, particularly process productivity.

Organizations are in business to get results—to deliver a quality product to a customer or consumers, to get it there on time and at a marketable price, and to make enough money in doing so to reward investors and to have some funds left to grow the business. Increasing process productivity, because of its relationship with size, effort, schedule, and defects, does engender these results. In Figure 12.4, we show the results

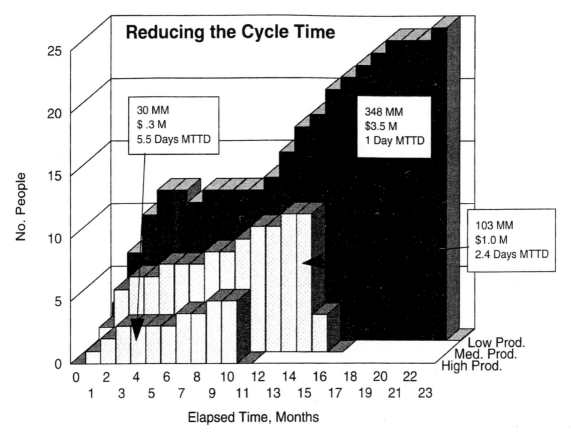

Figure 12.4 As process productivity increases from low in back to high in front, all the management numbers—the results—improve markedly.

that people can get by improving the software process. You can set this process in motion.

[1] C.K. Chang, "How to Solve the Management Crisis," *IEEE Software,* vol. 11, no. 6, Nov. 1994, p. 15.

[2] A.D. Hall, *A Methodology for Systems Engineering,* D. Van Nostrand Co., Princeton, N.J., 1962.

[3] G. Sharman, "When Quality Control Gets in the Way of Quality," *Wall Street J.,* Feb. 24, 1992.

[4] T. DeMarco and T. Lister, "Peopleware: Productive Projects and Teams," Dorset House Publishing, New York, 1987.

IEEE COMPUTER SOCIETY

Press Activities Board

IEEE Computer Society Publications

The world-renowned IEEE Computer Society publishes, promotes, and distributes a wide variety of authoritative computer science and engineering texts. These books are available from most retail outlets. Visit the Online Catalog, *http://computer.org*, for a list of products.

IEEE Computer Society Proceedings

The IEEE Computer Society also produces and actively promotes the proceedings of more than 141 acclaimed international conferences each year in multimedia formats that include hard and softcover books, CD-ROMs, videos, and on-line publications.

For information on the IEEE Computer Society proceedings, send e-mail to cs.books@computer.org or write to Proceedings, IEEE Computer Society, P.O. Box 3014, 10662 Los Vaqueros Circle, Los Alamitos, CA 90720-1314. Telephone +1 714-821-8380. FAX +1 714-761-1784.

Additional information regarding the Computer Society, conferences and proceedings, CD-ROMs, videos, and books can also be accessed from our web site at *http://computer.org/cspress*

1/29/99